Out of this World

Brendan Lloyd

Copyright © 2015 Brendan Lloyd

ISBN: 978-1-925442-06-9
Published by Vivid Publishing
P.O. Box 948, Fremantle
Western Australia 6959
www.vividpublishing.com.au

Cataloguing-in-Publication data is available from the National Library of Australia

All rights reserved. No part of this publication may be reproduced, stored in a retrieval system or transmitted in any form or by any means, electronic, mechanical, photocopying, recording or otherwise, without the prior written permission of the copyright holder.

Contents

La Réduction D'introduction	1
Otherworld Shown, Mind Blown (Experience '06)	6
Out 'There', In Here (Experience '08)	16
Believing Is Perceiving (Experience '11)	44
ESP, Yes Please	68
Conclusion Pour L'inclusion	85

La Réduction D'introduction

Bonjour ! I'm Brendan, and no, I'm not French, I hardly ever eat French food, and the most I normally have to do with anything French would be Ubisoft games, but since the French are fairly 'artistique' (artistic), I hope you appreciate me bringing a French flavour to this book, but I'll try to avoid sounding like Merovingian from the Matrix movies! I'm a writer, working on several diverse projects, however, at the time of writing this book, even though I have several completed projects, I haven't broken 'le charme de pas établi' (the spell of 'not established'), so if you're hoping for tips on how to break into 'the biz', there aren't many tips I can give you. Literally the only advice I can give you about 'breaking into the biz' with creative industries that will be any use to you is to find a person who is genuine : who has an eye/knack for predicting whether something will succeed or not (or spotting talent) and is rarely wrong, and who's willing to give you advice about what can be improved – i.e an executive type who is willing to give you a chance who won't turn you down immediately and be 'assez impitoyable' (fairly ruthless) because of being 'not established', but one who recognises whether you have potential or not, and if you're a musician, actor, or whatever, if there's anything wrong with your act, will give you positive feedback/constructive criticism, and if something 'needs work', will help you to fix and improve your act. Even having your own website is no guarantee.

I've written this book as a way of offering hope to those who are 'plus sceptiques' (more skeptical), and are looking for 'la preuve de Dieu' (proof of God), though if you're already interested in spirituality, and you've read plenty of 'alternative' books that the majority of people would take a look at the title or cover of and have no interest in reading, this book is for you, and you'll benefit more from it. I've tried to make this book as accessible as possible – don't worry if you normally think spirituality is lot of complicated jargon, you won't find 'New Age speak' in *this* book (well, you won't find *much* – just mentioning the word 'spiritual' is probably 'vague' and 'out there' enough for a lot of people)!

In this book, I'll by describing some spiritual experiences in '06, '08, and '11, and the details in this book aren't embellished, co-written, ghost-written, or fictionalised in any way, and are factual, based on my personal experiences, not second-hand accounts. Some details I don't remember – more happened than the details mentioned in later chapters, but I've only included what I remember. The 'experiences' described in later chapters have been a huge inspiration for creative projects, and have given me experience, inspiration, originality, etc with creative writing and overall maturity beyond what would normally be expected of a 27 year old.

You, the reader, don't have to 'believe' as such, but even if you *are* a sceptic or die-hard atheist, there are certain things that can't be explained by science, and require you to be open-minded. You might read this book once, think what I've described sounds ridiculous or unbelievable, and not gain much from this book, or it might confirm or back up some of the things you already believe.

I don't claim to be some 'all-knowing guru' who 'has all the answers' – there are some things I don't know, or with some of the things from my 'experiences', that I don't fully understand or don't remember. If you're a spiritual person looking for 'New Age' terms and concepts, you won't find much of that kind of content in this book, and if that's what you're looking for, then I'd suggest looking somewhere else.

I will present the information from my experiences in the most accessible way possible, and present the case that there is more than what we normally perceive. I feel like I've been 'lucky' to have had some intensely spiritual experiences that very few others have had, and I understand that for people who've had no experiences in their life that they couldn't explain or that they felt were spiritual and that for them, it's very difficult to believe in anything 'spiritual'.

If, for whatever reason, you were 'drawn' to this book – maybe it was the title, or the cover, or you walked into the 'alternative' section of a bookstore, picked this up, and read the blurb on the back, I hope this book benefits you and that you gain something from it.

Whatever you believe (or disbelieve), I hope the information presented in this book gives you something to ponder. I'll let the skeptics make their own conclusions, but I hope, if you're a skeptic, that you read this book from cover to cover, even if you only read it once, before you decide what to make of it. If you're already a spiritual person, I hope you find this book inspirational or '*inspiriti*onal*' if you prefer in some way (*which was initially an unintentional typo around 1 :30 pm on 28/5/15 that I only noticed later – one time I wrote 'soreceress' instead of 'sorceress').

Thank you for letting me get this introduction out of the way, which tends to be 'le plus' boring (the most boring or 'ultra boring') part of a book, and tends to be very 'verbeux' (long-winded). Even if I don't see a cent from this book, I'll be glad I wrote it (and if you're reading this, had it published!) and if this book makes you think more deeply about spirituality, or be more willing to consider it, I'll know that 'Je suis réussie' (I am successful), or if you don't mind, a 'réussie *Aus*sie' (read 'really useful Aussie' if you want a laugh at my expense).

If this is the first 'alternative' book you've ever read, I wouldn't be surprised – even just the title of some alternative books is enough to put off all but a small number of people – they don't create some of them to be accessible, and if you don't even know what the title of the book means or is about, how are people supposed to make sense of those books ? There is virtually no 'New Age speak' in this book, which I've made a conscious effort to avoid.

If you buy this book second-hand years after it's been published for dirt cheap, lucky you, for the price of a fast food meal, you've bought what I hope you'll find is an alternative 'page turner'. On the plus side, this book will be a lot healthier than that fast food meal you'd otherwise have spent the money on. I apologise if you *do* find this book second-hand and the cover is torn or pages are missing – I don't control the books, I only write. Maybe this book is the *write* stuff for you, maybe not. Keep reading – because *too right* is alright in *my* book !

Otherworld Shown, Mind Blown (Experience 2006)

Ah, 2006 – before 'good headspace' and 'spiritual' were even words in my vocabulary. Without exaggerating, it was the worst year of my life by far. How could what I now consider my earliest 'spiritual experiences' make for the worst year of my life? Let me give you some background...

It was Year 12, probably a 'stressant' (stressful) time normally, with plenty of stressin' about the future, but for me it was a living nightmare. Having 'Asperger's' – or 'Assburgers' as shows like South Park have been calling it, in my younger years I was exposed to feelings of isolation, of being 'different', unappreciated, lonely, lack of acceptance, and 'shame'. 'Love' was not a word or an idea that had meaning for me until '08 or '09.

Added to this, years earlier there was a girl at Primary School I was interested in, who I got off to a bad start with because of what I call 'the phone incident', and for several years afterwards, I was overcome with grief, guilt and depression. She went to a different high school, and I wasn't able to properly apologise or make up for what I'd done, which gave me strong feelings of unresolved guilt. The feelings of guilt were so overwhelming, I cried many times for several years afterwards. I lacked the confidence to have been able to ask her if we could have been friends, and would like to be able to contact her now and be friends. I've made peace with this incident since and have been able to find humour in it – for example, there's a Stevie Wonder song called 'I Just Called To Say I Love You', which is similar to what I said during the 'incident', and I can hear that song now and find it funny.

More recently, 'Let it Go' has been what I'm doing in relation to this incident and this person – 'letting go' of all the guilt, resentment, anything negative in relation to this person, and have been focusing on gratitude, forgiveness, lessons I've learned from her, and if this doesn't sound too 'far out, man', unconditional love. This 'girl' (whose name I've avoided using to protect her privacy) has given me enormous creative inspiration, I've written many notes/observations about her such as positive character traits, explored what about her made me feel 'drawn' to her, and working out what things I'm grateful for, and if she is reading this (she'll know who I am) – I'm sorry for what I put you through, and for not having the confidence to ask if we could have been friends, but in hindsight I've gained inspiration and learned some lessons thanks to you, and I'm grateful that we were able to meet. 'Merci beaucoup' (thank you very much) for the things that I mentioned, and please 'soyons amis' (let's be friends). I forgive you for not signing a yearbook and forgive you if at the time, because of the incident, you thought I was strange.

In '06 I had been seeing a psychiatrist who was pushing all sorts of 'medication' on me, including but not limited to Ritalin, and I remember (on Ritalin) feeling like a complete zombie and having no energy. I was also prescribed anti-depressants, which had a revolting smell and taste, and wasn't able to swallow them, so I didn't take them, and when I *did* take them, they didn't seem to 'help' at all. I was then labelled as 'non-compliant' (a little like being 'not established', only scarier!) and being threatened by something called a 'treatment order', labelled with probably half a dozen alleged 'mental illnesses' – depression, 'schizoid-affective' ('affective' what? 'It's Super Effective' from Pokemon ?) bi-polar, and I dare you to name anything else, I was probably 'diagnosed' as having it. The words 'Guardianship Board' also came up'. I was definitely having problems with the mental health system, or should it be mental *hell* system ? Either way, it was definitely mental ! And don't get Scientologists started on psychiatry - one of them might read this and decide to take action . Strange as it sounds, I agree with their objections to psychiatry. Scenes on TV of a 'patient' on a bed in a hospital being restrained by several 'guards' while a 'doctor' prepares an injection, I hate to say, are surprisingly accurate, but those particular experiences of the mental health system come later in the book.

Would it be a fair guess that right about here you're wondering how any of this 'stuff about the mental health system' is 'spiritual' ? Well, this is about to get interesting ! Spread throughout '06 were unusual experiences, and I can't describe where my head was at, but I'd say it was 'uncharted territory' (sorry, that one doesn't really sound better in French) – there were some very 'off' vibes, and there was very high 'l'activité mentale' (mental activity) and a lot of it *was* very 'mental' !

I can't remember what order the events I'm about to describe happened in, but I'll describe them the best I can.

I had many 'ESP' type experiences during '06 – I would see a lot of red, yellow, etc – I wouldn't describe it as 'seeing auras' or anything like that, just flashes of energy. I felt a lot of negativity with these 'flashes of energy' – there was nothing peaceful about them at all. It's difficult to describe the feelings, especially in my mind, but there were what felt like intense anger and hatred - the 'vibes' I felt, if you believe in ce genre de chose (that sort of thing).

Sorry to 'nerd out' for a while, but I remember seeing many Final Fantasy VII related 'videos' on my computer that I could find no evidence of afterwards – one where the character Tifa dies and the video seemed to be called 'Tifa Dies', one that said 'Ruby Weapon beaten in 7 seconds using a van', and possibly some others I don't remember. In the 'Tifa Dies' video, the character Tifa was killed by the main villain, which doesn't happen in the actual game (Final Fantasy 7). It seemed like an alternate plot, but I found no evidence of it.

With the 'Ruby Weapon beaten in 7 seconds using a van' video, I'm not sure what 'using a van' means – whether it means a camera van, or Vanir (a group of Norse gods), or something else entirely, but I do remember it being very strange. How that enemy in the game could be beaten by a camera van, I have no idea, and my other theory of 'van' being short for Vanir, doesn't make much sense either. Why would a 'Vanir' be fighting Ruby Weapon ? If there are other things 'using a van' could refer to, I'm not sure. The idea of some kind of delivery van being driven into that 'Boss' and only taking 7 seconds to beat it, seems very 'L.O. L' material. Maybe it was kind of parody, or otherwise meant to be humorous, I'm not sure, but it seemed extremely random.

There was another Final Fantasy-related ESP thing – also on my computer, I remember seeing this video of some kind of action figures and a line something like 'They're all separate, until now !', or 'They've all been separate, until now ! Now they come together !' and a title of something called 'Final Fantasy Finalised'. I remember the action figures seemed to be very clay coloured, and there wasn't much movement, only still shots of these 'action figures'. This was another thing I tried searching for online and found no evidence of. What these things mean, is difficult to say, but definitely suggests ESP – for the mind to 'make up' things like these doesn't seem very likely, and would seem like unusually specific things for the mind to 'make up'.

When I say, 'I could find no evidence', it means that I tried doing internet searches much later and finding no mentions or matching results online. When I Googled these, there would be no results, even with quotation marks.

Starting to sound 'interesting' ? But wait, there's more ! I vaguely remember a girl entering my room, and possibly something suggestive, but I don't remember because my head was somewhere 'out of this world'. What's 'out there' about this, is that I didn't contact anyone, and I wasn't able to find any evidence of it afterwards. I had no contact at all with 'the girl' I mentioned before, so I don't know if it was even her or not. Also, I don't remember being contacted by anyone later, so I can't explain what happened. Maybe it was some kind of 'spirit vistation' ('esprit visites' – even *that* sounds better in French !), I'm not sure (Spirit visitation is a phenomenon where people encounter a particular person in mysterious circumstances, then even if they try to track the person down, can't find them anywhere, like they've mysteriously disappeared, or maybe weren't actually a 'person' to begin with).

Whether it had been 'the girl', or someone else, I'm sure I would have heard something/had someone contact me to tell me what happened. This seems very strange because I heard nothing, and I can't be sure whether something 'out there' happened or not, and my head had crossed into 'open seas during a freak storm' territory – with emphasis on 'freak'. If you've heard the expression 'freaky deaky', this was 'sneak *peeky*' of something 'beyond' – and not the 'Bed, Bath and Beyond' kind of beyond either. The 'Beyond' section *I'm* talking about is one you'll want to stay away from.

I also remember of kind of 'CG-ish' ESP on computer, that I could find no evidence of later. There seemed to be what looked like some kind of TV show I'd never seen before that seemed familiar somehow. It had a visual style that seemed like some kind of 'spiritual CG', it definitely *didn't* look anything remotely close to live action. There was some kind of battle, characters being submerged beneath some kind of energy that looked almost like water, but with a vibrant, spiritual appearance which has a 'je ne sais quoi' (if I have to translate *this* one, you should think about taking a French class !) and to try to describe it would use words even more vague than 'vibrant'. Then there were two characters holding hands, and some kind of song being sung after the battle had ended – which seemed not that different to the style of song in some Final Fantasy games, but whatever this 'TV show' was, it wasn't Final Fantasy – that would just be about the closest I can get to describing the style of it.

I also remember some other 'spiritual CG' type stuff, like some blonde woman (? [spirit ?]) in a blue dress who seemed like they were filming a movie or something because she seemed to always be in the bathtub, and hearing some strange noises, that the closest I could describe them as would be 'clink clink'. She was fairly attractive, and there was nothing hostile or untoward about her, but I had almost no idea who or what she was, it was 'un mystère' (a mystery).

I also remember seeing what I describe as 'the beautiful Spirit' – I was seeing some kind of beautiful spiritual being (or what I assume it was), but only in glimpses. You know how I used the word 'vibrant' two paragraphs ago ? Well *this* was literally indescribable, not remotely close to 'live action' in appearance whatsoever. This 'spirit' had a kind of spiky blonde hair, was dressed in white, and seemed to have extremely vibrant flowers in its hair,. To describe the best I can *how* I was seeing it, it appeared like a portal had opened and I was seeing into another world, it appeared as though it was 'floating' above me. There was an appearance that was incredibly 'radiant' for lack of a better word - there is no way what I was seeing was anything made of matter, (which by comparison had/has a much duller, rougher, 'dirty' appearance, and definitely not 'radiant' !) – I've seen no kind of material energy that resembles what I saw in the slightest.

Also, this 'being' didn't appear what would normally be considered 'male', but didn't look particularly 'feminine' either, apart from the flowers in the hair. He/it looked what the Japanese call 'bishonen' ('beautiful youth') – which any RPG or Anime fans reading should have some idea of ! *Very* bishonen.

The flower looked to be fairly pinkish or red, I don't quite remember, and there seemed to be a glowing aura surrounding this 'spirit'. The aura seemed to be partly gold, partly white, and partly blue, and a reasonably balanced mix of those colours. I'm sorry that I'm not a very good drawer or painter – I'm more '*aut*istic' than '*art*istic' ! If I was, I could sketch or draw what I saw - a picture's worth at least a thousand words, so they say. And some 'pictures' are worth a whole lot more than a thousand *dollars* !

This 'being' or 'spirit' didn't say anything, but seemed to be looking at me. There was nothing film d'horreuresque (horror movie-esque) about it at all – there was no 'Exorcist vibe' or anything even remotely close - no feeling of negativity, fear, hostility or anything sinister about it at all, it just seemed to be watching me. It was relatively peaceful, it said nothing but there was something reassuring about these 'visions'.

This was one of the earliest 'confirmations' I've had of something there being 'something else', and as I mentioned, it was definitely something 'spiritual' – there was incredible 'l'activité mentale' and it was almost 'two worlds colliding', it was definitely something from another world – I've described it as best I can, but it's very hard to avoid using vague words like 'vibrant' or 'radiant', which to a skeptic would be right up there with the word 'spiritual' on their 'List of Words To Scoff At If Someone Mentions'.

While all of these things were happening, I was 'doing' (or should I say 'doing badly at '?) Year 12. School was impossible – you've probably heard the expression of 'being from another planet', to be more accurate, my head seemed like it was in another *dimension* or something – this book's called 'Out of This World', and that was definitely what it felt like !

That doesn't bother me, because the reassurance, especially of seeing the 'beautiful spirit', is a lot more important to me than my academic results, which must have fallen into a sinkhole, then fallen into a hollow centre of the earth. I've seen 'educated people' who, like I mentioned with the 'List of Words To Scoff At', would scoff at even saying the *word* 'spiritual', despite being well 'educated', weren't even open to anything that had any hint of spirituality and who seemed to act like a know-it-all because they had this or that piece of paper and who act like you have to have a 'piece of paper' to know 'rien à rien' (anything about anything). I try to avoid acting anything like them, because there are some things you can't talk about at all with people like that. I don't like being treated as though 'Je dois être stupide parce que je ne suis pas instruite' ('I must be stupid because I'm not 'educated''), and it makes me wonder what kind of 'education' it really is!

Even using the word 'Spirit' is probably 'as vague as', (for a laugh – Google the French translation of 'as vague as'), and 'vague as' is probably only useful when it's got 'Las' in front of it and is the name of a city. 'Spirit' is probably a word that either means something to you, or it doesn't.

I feel like saying 'but wait, there's more' again, because there's a *lot* still to cover. If there wasn't, there wouldn't be much between the covers, and I'd be ducking for cover rather than writing something to be *read* from cover to cover.

If this is starting to sound 'interesting', then it's about to get 'outta sight', unless you spoilt it for yourself by flipping ahead to later chapters – naughty you, (most) books don't come with a spoiler alert !

Out 'There', In Here (Experience '08)

'Out of sight, out of mind'…well, more like *'out of your mind'*. There's 'out there', then there's 'something going on here'. If what I've described in the previous chapter isn't 'interesting' enough for you, this is where things get 'OMG, maybe there *is* a 'My God' to say 'Oh' about'. And *not* the 'Oh, that's God's act? I was expecting quelque chose de plus mystérieux ('something more mysterious'). He's supposed to be all about 'mysterious ways', but his performance wasn't very mysterious' kind of 'Oh' – the disappointed 'oh…is that it?' of 'oh'.

If you need more convincing, *maybe,* just maybe, there's a *tiny* possibility you're an atheist and the word 'God' isn't in your vocabulary, except when it has the words 'There is no…' in front of it. If you are and you're reading this book, bravo (well done)! Unless you wrote some book or other, I think it was called 'God Confusion' or something, and if you're reading *that* book instead of *this* one,' êtes-vous sûr de cela?' ('are you sure about that ?') - maybe it's a *delusion*, but it just seems like one's about *something* and the other one's about…well, nothing.

These details are probably out of order, but then again, apparently the 'whole….(fill in the blanks) is out of order'.

One thing I remember strongly was what seemed like seeing 'créatures mythiques' ('mythical creatures'. I can't remember exactly, but I thought I saw something vaguely similar to a kitsune (Japan fans should know this one!) There seemed to be something like a sequence on some anime and games (usually an opening or closing sequence) where there are lots of characters on screen and they 'pop out', or seem like they're 'bursting' from the screen in all directions. Not, 'bursting at the seams' – that mostly happens to pairs of pants!

It's 'plus correct' (more correct) to say they were bursting from the *scene* in all directions.

'So what?', I was 'just watching anime', someone I know less about than a bar of soap's probably thinking. That *sounds* like scepticisme raisonnable ('reasonable skepticism'), but about that – first – I wasn't watching TV, second – I haven't seen any anime that looks like 'spiritual CG', and one other thing that blows a hole in that argument – remember the 'beautiful spirit' I said seemed like it was above me and I saw a portal or something and it seemed it 'seeing into another world'? Yes, *that* thing. Like that, this definitely seemed to be *above* me, and the 'bursting from the scene' thing I mentioned? How many Anime have I seen that seem like 'spiritual CG', seem to have 'créatures mythiques' appearing above me, and seem like seeing through a portal into another world? None yet, but if there *is* one, it's going on my 'Must Watch' list!

Anyone thinking this is starting to sound 'cool', I don't want to burst your bubble, because this was probably a hundred times more painful than recent seasons of Simpsons. 'Don't try this at home'! I will say that it was definitely 'Une Esper-ience' (bonus points if you know what that word means!)

The earliest thing I remember is being asked where the 'keys' were, and I said that I'd swallowed them. The keys were house keys, but I thought it was the keys 'Sin, Death and Hades', and believed I'd swallowed them. Whether this was 'l'affaire' (the case) or not, I don't know, but there's still a lot of 'sin' and 'death' out there – just turn on the news or le current affairs! Try telling me with a 'visage impassible' (a straight face) there's no 'sin' or 'death' on the news, and I'll be thinking *you're* the one being the comedian and asking 'why aren't you in standup ?'.

I also remember something about 'swallowing eggs' (not literally), and not knowing what it was. There was a moment where I felt like a snake swallowing a giant pearl or a pearl necklace – and I *can* be snaky sometimes, but thank 'God' I don't look like one!

While all this was happening, I felt a feeling of 'crystallisation' or something in my head, like my brain was some kind of crystal. It's very hard to describe the feeling, but if you've seen that Indiana Jones movie about the crystal skull, that's almost what it felt like in my head. I also saw a lot of some kind of 'reddish gold' colour ESP – and have no idea what it was. All that glitters ain't gold, but if it *is* gold, it ain't no 'gold rush' I've ever seen!

I also remember another ESP 'thing' (yes, apparently 'it's a thing') about 'Gog' and 'Magog' from the Bible passage Revelation 20:7-9 "And when the thousand years are finished, Satan shall be loosed out of his prison, and shall come forth to deceive the nations which are in the four corners of the earth, Gog and Magog, to gather them together to the war: the number of whom is as the sand of the sea. And they went up over the breadth of the earth, and compassed the camp of the saints about, and the beloved city: and fire came down out of heaven, and devoured them"

I remember having this theory I couldn't explain about Gog translating as 'Prince' and Magog translating as 'Great Prince' in *maybe* the language of the Biblical Philistines [if *any* written records or otherwise survive at all of that language to verify this] - I can't prove them being the correct translations though, maybe something was 'lost in translation' as they say!). For some reason I believed it was the 'Devil' fighting his 'Dark Side', where 'Gog' (the 'dark side') and Magog was his 'Light Side', and they were fighting each other.

I had a 'notion' of Samael (an alleged 'fallen angel' whose name, translated from Hebrew means 'Poison of God' - maybe it was the liquor kind of 'poison' – as in 'pick your poison' – and he likes to 'get wasted' a lot! Maybe he had a lot of '*wasted* potential' and should have been working in 'Waste Management'!) and 'Satan' being separate beings, that were going through a 'bitter separation'! Obviously if he'd ever heard 'Never Tear Us Apart', he was thinking the opposite – 'tear us apart straight away'!

I had a theory that by chanting 'Gog' (or should that be '*grog*'?) or 'Magog' (imagine a 'Deep South' accent saying 'quit touchin' *mah grog*!' or 'who's been touchin' *mah grog*?'), people put their support behind either 'Satan' or 'Samael' and whichever of the two 'rallied the most nations' would be the winner.

I had a feeling of 'Satan' and Samael being like evil and good halves respectively, and a feeling of the 'Devil fighting his Dark Side' – which in this case had nothing to do with Star Wars! But there was definitely a 'War' of some kind – it felt like this 'Samael', who in Kabbalah tradition has long been associated with the 'dark side of the Kabblah', the Qliphoth, and yes, right now most of you reading this would be thinking, 'whatda? Qliphoth? But I thought cliffhangers were meant for TV!'.

Some gamers will have heard of Sephiroth from Final Fantasy VII, Sephiroth is the 'Light Side' of the Kabbalah, and no, I'm not turning this book into a 'Kabbalah for Dummies' guide, but God knows we need one, because the words 'Kabbalah' and 'obscure things almost no one has heard of' have a long and stable marriage and should be giving out pamphlets for 'how to maintain a successful marriage'.

Again, this was seemed to be happening 'above' me, and while I've heard the expression 'As Above, So Below', there *is* such a thing as 'below acceptable standards', and humanity's history has too many examples to list. Do you want a free history lesson as well? In some countries they have free education, so there's your 'free history lesson', of course, it probably comes from a textbook and you'll probably only have an intellectual understanding of the history lesson's significance, and I hope you're not in a hurry to re-enact it – hands up, who wants another Hitler? Actually, don't answer that one – the original one already take a few *hits* in the sanity department. Someone should have sat him down in a psychiatrist's chair – and put him at the top of their 'Mental Health *Hit*list'.

I seem to remember a very psychotic voice saying 'I will destroy this vehicle' and not knowing what kind of 'vehicle' this voice was talking about, or even who the voice was. It sounded extremely demonic, maybe for all I know, it could have been Ahriman from Zoroastrianism, who knows, because Angra Mainyu is one angry dude! Unless you've seen Hercules (the live action show with Kevin Sorbo), and have recently watched season 5 on DVD, you're probably thinking 'Zoroastrianism? Is Legend of Zorro creating its own religion now?', or maybe not, but you'd be forgiven for not knowing much about it.

Suffice to say, if you've heard of the Mazda car brand, take a wild guess where the name 'Mazda' comes from, or look it up on Wikipedia. I won't spoil the 'moment of realisation' that comes with finding something out for yourself, otherwise it'd be a 'moment of reading a book that tells you something unrelated to the topic of the book just to see how clever you are', and then probably, if you don't know, a book telling you 'you might want to read up about this, just saying'. Do many books do that? Probably not, but they weren't brought to you by 'manic brilliance', although I don't think Robin Williams had quite that kind of 'manic' in mind.

I have of collection of Egyptian god figurines from a magazine, and I remember lining them up, as if to decide which ones were 'on my side'. I guarantee if you've ever watched Stargate, you could name some of them, and there would be some others that you'd pass if I was giving a quiz. Some can't get enough of Egyptian cotton – to them I say 'Egyptian cotton? How about Egyptian gods? Because you know that if they exist, they probably created that Egyptian cotton'.

One time I went to the shops and heard a voice ask me something about Meretseger (a goddess figurine, one of the figurines), and it sounded like they were about to make a phone call. I'm not sure who it was, or who they were going to 'make the call to', but if it's 'out of this world', I've either experienced it, or know what you're talking about. Trust me, if you think *you're* into anything 'obscure', I redefine the meaning of obscure.

While lying in bed, with my mind 'crystallising', I remember hearing several voices saying 'Magog, Magog' and 'rallying' around me, and then later starting a chant that went something like 'Se-ra-phim', and one of the voices (who may have been Japanese) chanted "Se-re-fu" (the same word in Japanese). I think the chant was to give the Seraphs the power/morale to fight against the Devil's forces.

Assuming you believe chants and mantras have power, remember – atheists aren't exactly the world's most logical people. Do I need to drop the 'Dawkins' bomb? No? Good. If Richard Dawkins is considered 'logical' for dismissing even the slightest hint of religion or spirituality, then God (assuming he exists, according to an atheist's *dis*belief system) help us all!

Anyone who believes in angels has probably one or twice heard a few names and words, but if you haven't heard of Cherubim and Seraphim, remind me never to ask for your book on angelology, a word that sounds only slightly better in French, even with the accent.

There was a time when I would have questioned the existence of angels, but given what I've seen and experienced, just because something is invisible, doesn't mean it's not there. Science has proven the existence of many types of light invisible to the naked eye (e.g infrared, x-rays) that can only be seen with goggles, which before being discovered, people would naturally have assumed did not exist, but now if a person were to say infrared and x-rays 'don't exist', we'd probably think they were let out of the 'loony bin' too soon, or weren't put in one in the first place and need to go there!

I've been in a 'loony bin' several times, and I'll say it gets easier each time. Sure, you're treated as a criminial by psychiatrists who literally only care whether a person's taken medication and nothing else about a person, but hey, it's not like anyone's ever said anything bad about them…Oh wait, they have said bad things about psychiatrists and they're called 'Scientologists', which makes no sense as a title – "Scientology = Study of Science (Fiction)". They probably could have picked a slightly better name for themselves – 'study of science'? Yeah, but which one?

Back to this Satan/Samael 'duality' for a moment – it felt like the 'Satan' part was inside me (in my head, and no, don't say 'it was all in my head'), and that I was 'overcoming him', to the point where it felt like this 'entity' tried to break free (with pain shooting through my back). I believed I 'forced him to Sheol' before he broke free - I've heard the Queen song 'I Want to Break Free', but someone could have warned me HE was trying to break free! I want to break free as well – break free from this strange 'thing' called material existence, which is obviously God's 'work in progress'.

Don't ask when he'll be 'finished' – God, like the Devil, is one for details, even more meticulously, but didn't get his own expression, and he doesn't like 'being bothered during work hours'. Try contacting God on a Sunday, that's his rest day, and he's usually a cool customer, whoops, *you're* the customer, God's the one running the operation. It's a great operation he's got going, he just has to deal with 'devils in the wiring'.

I remember walking around, believing I was saying what 'Satan' tells God in Book of Job (Bible) after God asked him where he had been, and that everything leading up to the 'End Times' was like a video game or a play, and that when I spoke, it was like a deep 'demonic' (think Goa'uld voice in Stargate) and remember saying thing like the things the serpent in Genesis (the Garden of Eden section) and using my hand to imitate the mouth of the serpent, like a sock puppet with a dirty, stinkin' sock on my hand, and who wants to wear a stinky sock on their hand? It's bad enough when people have them on their feet!

With all the crystallisation in my head, when I walked around, it felt is if earthquakes were being simulated, as though to imitate the effects of a several hundred metre tall giant walking around, and I felt *I* was the giant. I've heard sometimes you can 'feel the earth, move, under your feet', but this was something else. Who *was* this giant, and why did I believe the giant and I were one and the same?

It was a strange feeling, like I was 'stomping around', and yes, I've heard the expression 'stomping grounds', but it felt like I had assumed the identity of the 'Devil' and everything relating to the 'End Times' was carefully scripted, and the Devil had to follow a certain strict set of guidelines or he'd be punished.

The 'Devil' was playing some kind of game with God, and the game involved certain rules. You're probably thinking the idea of a 'Devil' playing by anyone's rules but his own is a strange concept, but reality TV is a stranger concept in my book – if the 'Devil's in the details', then he must be off the hook for reality TV, because they don't hire writers or actors and they make everything up on the spot, including their explanation for why people watch TV calling itself 'reality' that's obviously playing the melodrama for ratings. Have any concepts stranger than that? Then you must be more into anime and RPGs than I am – Japan is the unofficially the world's most creative country. Yes, I know, U.S, but let's face it, of all the shows they have promos for, I'm lucky if even one is a 'keeper'.

The terms of the 'game', as I understood them at the time were outlined by the Bible and the reward was a 'lamb' – a reward with no strings attached, provided that the game was played through to its end. I interpreted the purpose of 'the game' as being to teach the Devil about love, sacrifice, redemption, etc. In this 'interpretation', he was still a villain, but one who could 'work with God' rather than against him, and was self-aware (aware of his own reputation), and had an interest in exploring cette facette de lui-même ('this facet of himself') with humanity. Look, I just used the word 'meme' – internet memes would be just what a Devil would want, just don't give him the details, he's very particular that way.

Whether these interpretations are 'truth' or not is irrelevant, this is how I interpreted them at the time.

The picture I had at the time of the Devil, as in 'during manic mode', which doesn't come with an 'off switch', was of a selfish 'son of God' who wanted everything but didn't want to earn it, so 'God' decide he could 'learn it' instead. Almost like employment – some believe you either have to 'earn' or 'learn', but if you're earning, you're not learning, and if you're learning, you're not earning. There should be a 'having fun' and 'being a good person' in there somewhere, but the Bible wasn't proofread by a guru, just Catholic priests. And by 'proofread', I mean...wait, are we having this conversation? Whoops, no way that's getting past the censors.

Through this 'game', 'sin' would be destroyed when the Devil 'died' or in Christian language, 'became dead to sin' (or from my point of view and belief at the time, when *I* died), because 'sin' was within his own body, it was the 'Devil's' job to redeem himself by destroying sin. 'Sin' in this sense was not so much related to behaviour as a type of 'contamination within the body', and when he 'died', the last record of 'sin' would have been destroyed and that would mark the beginning of the 'End Times'.

Keep in mind, this was my 'manic mindset' at the time, and I don't think in terms of Christian 'End Times' anymore. If I see an evangelical Christian channel on 'cable', I just keep looking until I find something I actually *want* to watch. If you (the reader) on the other hand for reasons unknown to me have a fascination with evangelical Christians 'preaching the gospel' who, despite there being plenty of other books of the Bible, focus unusually heavily on Revelation, it's funny how strongly they believe in the end of the world instead of, you know, actually having faith that things can improve. 2012 didn't happen, but those guys didn't get the 'end of the world is a bust' memo!

After that, or maybe before that, I remember sweating heavily and it felt like something invisible was floating around the room trying to attack me with invisible energy blasts, in a similar style to Dragon Ball Z. This être caché ('hidden being') seemed familiar and seemed to remind me of someone.

I remember hearing one voice say something like 'Stop it, you're hurting him', and seemed to be having a conversation with the être caché, who at one point said something like 'I can't, he's still using it to get around' (which I interpreted as talking about my body). I told this être caché that 'there is another way', and it stopped attacking me just like that.

While the invisible "being" was flying around, a Naruto Shippuden movie had a plot involving ten shadowy guys firing Dragon Ball Z-style energy blasts at Naruto and killing him. After the 'being' stopped attacking me, the Naruto Shippuden movie's plot had mysteriously changed to one where Naruto had to fight a devil-style character and his "death" was a vision.

I also remember being on the floor on all fours and raging, still with my mind feeling 'crystallised' and mentioning 'Ten Tailed Beast' which later appeared in Naruto Shippuden's plot.

One voice said to me 'You look very beautiful in your true form', but at the time I didn't know what they meant, or who was saying it, only that she reminded me of the girl from Primary School.

One time at the shops, I heard voices talking in a way that people don't usually talk in. Instead of them saying somebody had died, they said they were 'in the etheric', or something like that, and one voice said something about an 'infinity mind', which I understood to mean either my own mind or God's mind. Another voice (who I called 'Zack') said something about something "being within reach" or something like that, which at the time, I took to mean the End Times.

Clairaudience (another French word), or for the non-French speakers, 'clear hearing' (otherwise known as 'hearing voices') is not new to me, and isn't limited to manic experiences. Of course, I'm not telling a psychiatrist that I 'hear voices', I think you can guess what the outcome of *that* would be. It's probably bad enough telling them you see 'dead people', which rules out the kid from the movie Sixth Sense seeing a psychiatrist.

I remember a voice saying extremely derogatory things, I think it was the same voice that said 'I will destroy this vehicle'. It seemed like a demonic entity trying to attack me, and I never learned who or what it was, but 'getting to know demons' is not the raison d'etre of a spiritual experience. Getting to know your *inner* demons, maybe, but you might want a psychologue (psychologist) for that. They call them *psycho*-logists for a reason – if you have psyche (sorry, that's a Greek word, not French) issues (and face it, most of us do), they're a logist (read : logical person) who can help you, and won't ask you to pop any pills.

At one point, I remember holding my throat and feeling a burning feeling inside, which at the time felt like I was 'burning the Devil's sin' and only leaving behind records of the things he had done throughout history. A throat lozenge may have helped with the burning sensation, but you just don't think about these sorts of things while things, if anything you do too much thinking – if you've heard the expression (probably paraphrasing) 'Don't think, it'll hurt your brain', now you know what it means. If there is one thing that describes manic to a T, it's 'brain pain'.

I was talking incessantly through the whole experience, calling myself 'the Devil's body of excess karma' and 'the Devil's sin container', and it felt like inside my body was a collection of scrolls (and no, not the Elder Scrolls) and that I was 'burning' the Devil's sin. As the sins were being 'burned', the scrolls were being opened. If you think scrolls are 'old fashioned', try 'scrolling' down a web page using neither a mouse nor arrow keys. If you're using a laptop, no cheating by using the touch pad !

I had an 'interpretation' of the Devil being like the Titans (Greek mythos) and that he was the most powerful member of a race similar to the Titans, though far greater in number, which I believed were the notorious 'Nephilim' (meaning 'fallen ones' in Hebrew, believed to be half-angel, half-human) and that 'Satan' was the leader of these 'demons' and was trying to lead an attack against angels.

There also seemed to be throwbacks to Lord of the Rings, in the sense that it felt like 'Satan' had a ring that bound the other 'giants' to this will and was able to enslave other races as well. The 'Satan' that I seemed to sense seemed very similar to Sauron, and was preparing his forces for an attack against angels. On the other hand it seemed like 'Satan' was the

Dark Side' of Samael, who had separated in a less than friendly way from this 'Dark Side' and was working to defeat 'Satan' once and for all.

At one point there were these strange 'survival' sorts of things, where it was a sort of 'how long can a male and female survive in a cold environment for' type thing that had (I assumed) something to do with evolution or something like that (yes, I said 'evolution' – get used to it !) and certain members of each ethnic background would hide in a certain place, like a cave (yes, I know, this is being set up for a 'cavemen' reference) in the event that humanity was faced with extinction and would repopulate from the two people of that ethnic group.

There was something about saying a particular prayer to keep themselves alive and there were prayers to 'Jehovah' and various other names I can't remember, but it was praying to 'Yahweh' that kept them alive.

I remmber something about an 'air language' and around that time I started talking in a hybrid Nordic/Russian accent and believed I was speaking 'Lufian'. I'm not sure what an 'air' language is, because I'd assume any language that was spoken was an 'air language', but perhaps it was some kind of magic (which besides being a Queen album, may be some kind of magical language). Une touche de magie est enchanteur ('a touch of magic is enchanting'), unless you think magic is evil, in which case, you'd read it as 'being touched by magic is a form of enchantment'.

I also remember something early on that seemed like Hitler on a death bed dictating (yes, I know, he was well known for doing that) memoirs to be typed at, and it seemed like Eva Braun was typing the notes (at this point I was starting to believe I was a reincarnation of Hitler). I can't remember the content of the notes, but it seemed like Hitler (or at least me talking as though I was 'talking through Hitler' or the opposite) was describing beautiful things in the world, include people who were beautiful, and they were his last words or something. He sounded broken, and seemed like he was trying to leave the world with some kind of positive contribution and was remorseful and he regretted his life.

What the real significance of this was, Je ne sais pas ('I don't know'), but I feel even to this day, in light of the recent discovery of archival footage of the Queen at age seven giving a Nazi salute, that not enough has been done to achieve 'de-nazification', whether within Germany itself, or in other countries. For example, there needs to be more novateur ('innovative') creative works that bring something new and positive (not limited to comedy) to 'The Nazi Legacy'. The recent situation with the archival footage highlights this problem and shows a décevant ('disappointing') lack of awareness of the degree of trauma and 'guilt by association' that is involved, especially for Germans.

I remember showering with my clothes on and doing something to do with phonetics – I was talking in an unusual way as though I was trying to 'wash out my mouth' of the current languages and to 're-translate' certain languages and 'rewrite'. There was a point where I was speaking some unidentitied language had some relation to Latin, but I can't remember what I said. I've heard of washing your mouth out with soap if you have bad language, but what happens when the bad language is actually bad languages? I can understand washing out German – especially the words 'nein', 'heil' and 'fuhrer' (any objections?), but I have nothing against French, Spanish or Italian as languages, apart from the pretentiousness of the Merovingian character from the Matrix movies.

I remember there be being what seemed like some sort of god that had given up most of his powers to teach the world things and also to find some prophecy. When he found out about this 'prophecy', he reacted like 'What is this prophecy ? I must have that prophecy at any cost'. It seemed like he had divided his power so he could search through different realities until he found 'the prophecy', and also to 'clean out' certain junk from each reality as he went, regaining more and more of his power as he progressed. He *did* seem to have similarities to Voldemort from Harry Potter, but seemed to be a god rather than a human, and substantially less evil.

 It seemed this god was trying to create something to take away people's fear of death, and God had made an 'Elder Wand' with which he could create anything he needed, and which would allow him to divide his soul an almost unlimited amount of times until he had finished 'searching realities' for the mysterious 'la prophétie'. What this prophecy was about, or why he was so anxious to find it, I'm not sure, but it must have had a qualité indispensable ('an indispensable quality').

I never gained a sense of this 'god's name, but he seemed familiar. In a sense, with his 'reality searching', he was a kind of dieu des lacunes ('god of the gaps'), though he was not creating the gaps, he was trying to bridge them.

When this 'god', as a mortal, died, his soul would still be in many pieces, but besides clearing negativity and lies from particular realities, the power of amour pur ('pure love') also helped to restore his power. Through the many things he had seen, he gained a more complete understanding of pure love, and to paraphrase, 'Better Man', he was 'doing all he could, to be a better god'.

This 'god' seemed to be attempting to join alternate realities together, as each one was like a 'fragment' of our world which the 'Devil' had caused to separate from ours through lies and deception. But this didn't seem to be the only motivation for him, he seemed to want to glimpse into the 'vie après la mort ('afterlife', see how much better that sounds in French ?) in order to ease people's fear of death. In each way that he was similar to Voldemort, there were as many, if not more, ways he was different. For one, he was motivated by compassion and wisdom rather than self-interest, and he had little regard for his own safety.

I remember having a feeling that many fictional things were linked together in some grand way, and fictionalised certain events that all took place, but in a different reality. It brings to mind an expression, 'Every myth has a grain of truth', but I'll go 'one further' and adapt this expression to creativity, and in French. 'Toute fiction a once de vérité' ('Every fiction has an ounce of truth'). I didn't use 'grain', because that's an old expression, and 'ounce' sounds more substantial than a 'grain' – when I hear 'grain', I think a *grain* of rice, or a *grain* of sand, an ounce at least is a decent amount and sounds more 'precise'.

I had a sense of some things representing actual things, which people assumed were fictional, but were fictionalised (a fictional account of actual events or characters), meaning that although the works contained fictional characters, some of the events had some basis, but some of them may have only been in an alternate reality, a situation of la vérité est relative ('the truth is relative').

I remember believing that things like Stargate were 'real', or at least that things like the Goa'uld were real and were 'serpent seed' and also that the Ori were real, but were in reality the opposite of how they were portrayed in Stargate. For example, they were holy and seemed to be true gods, not some kind of 'ascended being', and their religion was unlike anything we had on Earth – almost an amalgamation of Earth's religion that despite incorporating 'pagan' traditions, still worshipped only a single God, believed in things like reincarnation, recognised our origins, especially in Christian countries were pagan traditions had been suppressed, and they had sent messengers, similar to Priors to warn us of the threat posed by the evil aliens (the Goa'uld-like aliens), some of which were 'hiding among us' (possibly the origin of some reptilian theories).

I remember believing the 'aliens' were planning to invade Earth and that the beings that I equated with the Ori had the only 'true' religion that acknowledged all religions, but we interpreted them as being evil, and interpreted as they were portrayed in Stargate. Unlike the Stargate Ori who I interpreted as a caricature, this did not anger them, but instead increased their determination to free us from the evil aliens by turning to the internet.

They were not 'hung up' on the idea of being worshipped and had a very humourous take on religion, and were amused by their portrayal in Stargate. They treated the 'stars' as sacred, having an almost Mario Galaxy-like interpretation of 'the stars', and recognised the implications of their portrayal on Stargate, seeming to prefer creative people who were open to new ideas and concepts and avoided people who were materialistic or had a rigid mentality. They also had loose ideas of what counted as mental health, for example, 'manic experiences' did not count as mental illness in their views, while being greedy or power-hungry was considered péché mortel (a 'mortal sin'). Strange how the French word for 'sin' sounds like peach, don't you think? Does this mean eating peaches is a sin ? How are we going to tell all the lovers in the world that peaches are sinful ? They'll have to find a *new* romantic food.

I remember experiencing things that seemed like they were from alternate realities, like a genetic disease that I can't remember the name of that was like widespread amnesia, and that the people suffering from this disease seemed as though they lived in a different reality (as in, the Many-Worlds Theory) and I was seeing into *their* reality.

It felt like I was a member of a band in one of those realities, but I don't know what its name was or how successful they were. I also remember hearing people tralking about the end of the world, including one voice who said something like 'what's the point of buying a new house when the world's going to end' or similar, and there was a widespread fear the world was ending in this alternate reality. 'End of the world' *does* sound better in French - la fin du monde, but saying 'end of the world' in any other language isn't going to make it any stressful.

One person seemed almost like a priest saying what kind of 'blessings' he woke up to, like butter and toast, and another person who thought I was trying to destroy their reality. I told the people of this alternate reality that all I was doing was cleansing many years of accumulated negative energies – some but not all of it created by demons, and that by holding my throat I was blocking the 'source' of the negative energy (going back to that 'the Devil inside' theme) and acting as a sponge to absorb it. You can call me a 'sponge' (i.e not having a traditional job, education or relationship) if you want, but it's just water off a duck's back to me. (Bonus points if you got the reference I made)

At one point, it felt like the Titans (Greek mythology – breaking the thème français, but 'manic doesn't conform to a specific language'. Is that an acceptable enough excuse ?) had been released from Tartarus and they didn't know very much, being trapped there for so long prevented them from experiencing very much. I felt like I was teach things – for example, they seemed to have limited understanding of 'spiritual laws', 'love' and 'time' – in fact, it felt like time was either almost forzen still or racing and alternating between the two, so it felt like I had to teach them how time operates. They also seemed to not understand the concept of 'tough love', so I felt I had to teach them that as well. I explained in more detail what 'tough body of love' meant. Looking at it now, I think 'tough body of love' was similar to Buddha nature, but had to be 'dumbed down' for a Titan audience.

With spiritual laws they seemed to not understand God, or how he could be everywhere, so I had to teach them about alternate dimensions and whatnot. I settled on an explanation close to animism. The one thing to keep in mind with spiritual laws, is that if you break them there's a much higher penalty if you break 'ordinary laws'. If you've heard the expression 'that's a matter for the courts', I like to change it to 'a matter for *God's* courts', because you know God is going to be a fairer judge than a middle age man wearing a wig. There's a movie called

Remember the Titans, and after all that, I'll be 'remembering the Titans' for a long time to come!

I saw at one point some kind of character wearing a bandana, who appeared almost like the 'beautiful spirit' I mentioned in the last chapter, but I had no idea who he was.

At one point, I heard voices that sounded like they were on the radio, that seemed like particular gods from mythology and they were talking about various things, and saying that I hadn't given them many scripts to work from. It also felt like some guy called Mark) was an avatar of the character Sephiroth and that he was like law enforcement (in relation to God) and that if someone did something bad, he 'harmed their mark' writing what they had done in a black book.

I was communicating with (what seemed) this other reality, and as I was talking, it sounded like what I was saying was being recorded (in the "alternate reality") and I was saying things like 'Inner Ain Soph' (which was really the mind's eye) and something about a 'U3' Ain Soph (whatever that means, I thought it was a group, one male and two females, who loved each other [well, the females loved the male and vice versa] that had different personalities but they complemented each other. I'm not sure if this is an expression or not, but 'l'étranger le nom, l'étranger la bande' (the stranger the name, the stranger the band).

It was like the Sephiroth (the ones from the Kabbalah) recorded good deeds in a white book and the Qliphoth recorded bad deeds in a black book. Fun fact: some people put telephone numbers in a black book. So black books aren't just hitlists.

Another thing I remember about is people who said something like "He wants us to come back and get that part of him when we're finished". I assumed that that meant coming back to take me to Heaven, and by "that part" they meant the part of me that was here in my body. Still waiting for that to happen, not sure when these people are meant to be finished whatever it is they're doing, but I guess it won't be for a while yet.

Someone who sounded like the same person (who I didn't know who they were, so I just called him Zack after the character from FF7) saying something like "You're missing the point of Advent Children entirely"'. I'm not entirely sure even now what the point of AC was, I have a few ideas though, but I guess what I thought back then wasn't right.

I think the people who sounded like they were on the radio referred to Bono as 'Seth' and insulted his ability to sing (unless they meant someone else), which I replied to with something lik e 'It's not his voice that matters, but what he sings about'. At one point while talking in the 'Lufian' accent, I was talking about Loki and some other god, who were both tricksters, and telling them to play pranks and practical jokes (which they specicialised in) and just to improve. I remember saying that there would be 'pandemonium in hell when Loki returned' or something along those lines. 'Returned' from what, I'm not sure, but it definitely wasn't to pick up drive through fast food. Gods eating fast food? Bien sûr, si elles veulent se faire passer pour l'homme ('Sure, if they want to pass for humans') Sure, Loki probably eats at Force of Norse.

I was thinking about a concept of "the same soul divided and contrasted". That was before I learned about what the Ain Soph really was, I thought it meant "one light' and was another name for God (although if the first word was changed to the German 'Ein' it would mean one light). On the subject of "one light", at one point I was singing the song one, but changed the lyrics, instead of the line "One love, one life" I sang "One love, one light, when it's one need in the night. One love, we get to share it, it leaves you baby if you don't care for it'.

So I was interpreting the "one light" being God's light and the one love also being God's love (although, it probably makes sense in some ways). At this point in was talking in the accent. I think I was singing some other songs as well, including Christmas Carols I think.

It felt like I was on the news, and I could hear people coming and going and (in response to the things I was saying) saying things about the end of the world and things like that.

There are some other things as well that I can't quite remember, but I think just before I went into hospital there was something to do with mermaids or something and a thing where it felt like the demonic entity was trying to kill me. But hey, what doesn't kill you, permanently cripple you, or weaken you in some way makes you stronger, right?

At one point I heard voices saying "keep talking" so I kept talking about various subjects, and after two weeks of manic, an ambulance arrived to take me into hospital. Before being taken away, I remember the same voice as a 'true form' line say 'The Creator has a purpose for you now', which at the time seemed strange – it suggested that up to that point I didn't have a purpose, then the Creator (or "God") decided to 'run with it'. That, and the paramedics decided to *run* me to hospital.

I spent six weeks in hospital, but I'll keep this short for the sake of reducing boredom. The boring bits were mostly in hospital – that's right, I called hospital boring – is that a crime?

When in hospital, I felt like I was no longer the sin container, that the container for cigarette butts was the sin container, so I was trying to pull it off the wall. And the cigarette butts in the grass to me presented extremely sinful people, and I put them in that drain, and it was like the drain was Sheol. I also remember trying to pull out the 'weeds from the Garden', the Garden representing to me the Garden of Eden, and saying that there were weeds in the Garden from the beginning (I considered the 'weeds' to be evil gods).

The hospital itself, in the 'closed ward', felt felt like a kind of Sheol as well, but not the same Sheol that the Devil, Beast and False Prophet were banished to or were to *be* banished to, but like a 'Sheol on Earth' type of place, and that by spending that time in that place I was 'repaying my debts' so that my sins could be forgiven and to free as many people as possible from being sent to the real Sheol at the End Times. It felt like an unearthly place. One part of it, passing through a long tunnel, felt very strange at the time, like entering a spaceship.

I *was* locked in a padded room at one point, but there was no strait jacket. I experienced a lack of compassion from the hospital/mental health system – I felt I was treated as a nuisance or inconvenience.

After the six weeks, I returned home and started becoming more open to things I hadn't considered before, and over the following three years, began looking into 'alternative' books, meditation, and Eastern religion. I began using the terminology 'manic experience' for what I'd been through to put a positive spin on my 'experiences' and felt a huge sense of release by doing this.

But this was only one part of my journey, and probably le plus difficile ('the most difficult'). There is still plenty more to come, and I don't want to brag (or maybe I do), but the 2011 experience was 'interesting' to get away with saying as little about it as possible before the next chapter.

I hope you're enjoying this book, it has been a journey for me to get myself ready to write it. Profiter de la livre ! ('enjoy the book')

Believing Is Perceiving (Experience '11)

If believing is perceiving, then it probably helps to believe something that isn't deceiving – either yourself or someone else.

I joke, but if you've heard the expression 'seeing is believing', I've reversed it – that believing is the first step to perceiving 'out there' things. Ever noticed how the people who say nothing 'spiritual' has ever happened to them tend to not believe in ESP or 'out there' things to begin with?

Coincidence? Maybe, but then 'they' (in 'spiritual circles') say that there's no such thing. But then the term 'spriritual circles' is probably loose as a goose to begin with, and bound to be misunderstood by at least the *occasional* Deep South preacher.

From 2010 to March 2011 was a time of intense creativitiy for me – several new projects had their beginnings in 2010, and 2011 manic only added to the creativity.

About three major creative projects of mine began in 2010 in some form, and this is 'ni le temps ni le lieu' ('neither the time nor place') to discuss projects, but no period before or since 2010 has been as creative in terms of ideas and concepts for new projects.

2011 Manic was notable for several reasons, especially for being so different to the previous one. It was as though manic had moved to another country, started speaking another language, and had a complete wardrobe change to go with it. To be honest 'go with it' is exactly what I did, because you don't control manic, it controls *you,* and it likes to keep you in suspense about what will happen next.

One thing a 'manic experience' is very good at is keeping you in suspense. You really have no idea what will happen next until it, well, happens, and probably happens to be something you weren't expecting. If you *are* expecting, I'd say being ready to leave for the hospital at a moment's notice is probably the best advice I can give.

So what was so special about 2011 manic? 'Probably just more of the same', you're probably thinking. Actually, it was closer to none of the same, because if 2011 manic counted as 'more of the same', then you must consider every Mario game to be 'more of the same', and stopped playing them years ago. If every life's a journey, then manic must be a journey into uncharted territory, with a broken compass and a book about spirituality with pages torn out your only guides in this 'magical manic wonderland'.

One thing I remember very clearly were some internet and computer ESP and strange headlines in the paper – and when I say 'strange headlines', I mean 'out of this world'. I remember all sorts of headlines ranging from Middle Eastern beliefs such as Djinns, to an article that was warning about doomsday prophecies that were focused on creating fear, which contained the warning "Beware doom and gloom prophets". There were other articles and headlines as well, including one that seemed like it was addressing me and saying I needed help.

I remember seeing several different things on internet and computer, such as for some kind of spirit whose name changed several times. First it was Matka Gabia, then it was Matika Gababa, then it become Matika Gaba and stopped changing. On the computer, I saw an image of an African or Aboriginal woman who was standing upright with some kind of pet, which looked to be a gryphon next to her and in the image, she was touching the gryphon's head as though to pet it.

The image was titled 'Matika Gaba and the Sly Griffin', but when I tried to look it up after 2011 manic, I found no evidence of it at all. I tried Googling 'Matika Gaba' in quotations, and found zero results. This was not a name I had seen in any book or video game at all, and the fact that Googling it returned zero results either tells you – I'm making it up and am being very upfront about it, or that some form of 'out of this world' knowledge was shown to me, and because of it having an 'otherworldly' origin, there was no record of it on the internet.

I don't know who or what this spirit (?) is, my theory is either an African or Aboriginal spirit or goddess, but if it is a goddess, I don't know what language the name is from, or what she is a goddess 'of'. If information having an 'otherworldly' source can be revealed to you with no record of it on the internet, it makes you wonder what other things are possible that skeptics over the years have deemed impossible.

I've heard of having a 'spiritual connection', and while I'm all for being in contact with 'gods' or 'goddesses', I'd like to at least know the significance of said 'spiritual connection' so that I 'know who I'm dealing with'…or not dealing with, because I don't who it is. That isn't 'not dealing with' in the sense of 'not dealing with issues', that's 'not dealing with' in the sense of not having further contact because I don't know who this spirit/goddess/whatever is or why they 'dialed in', but I might have to ask them to 'hold the phone' next time.

The presence of a griffin in the imagery is unusual because a griffin is not usually considered African or Aboriginal in the least sense, since they're normally considered Greek, and it's one of the few situation where it *isn't* 'all Greek to me'. I'm also not sure of the significance of the new 'Sly Griffin', but hopefully whoever or whatever he/she/it is, it's sly in a good way, rather than a bad way – sly as in clever rather than sly as in cunning.

I have found no mention of this 'goddess' anywhere online or in any books, assuming it is a goddess to begin with, but the imagery seems to match other imagery I've seen of depiction of gods and goddesses. I know very little about this subject – I literally only have the name and the images I saw, and nothing else to go on.

There was nothing hostile or untoward about this 'goddess' in any way, if anything it was more mysterious than anything else. If you're about to say 'this is starting to sound like a mystery school', I'll have to stop you there, because I don't consider myself a member of any mystery school, and I think if they wanted people to join them, calling it an école de mystère ('mystery school') is about as mysterious as you can be, and doesn't exactly do much for their image. It's not hard to imagine that only a few hundred years ago, 'mystery school' would have meant something like 'Satanic cult' or 'pagan cult' to the majority of people - if not in name, then by the nature of its secrecy.

You may have heard of how Native Americans mention 'the Spirits' quite a bit and maybe you're one of the more sceptical kind of people who thought they were strange for talking about 'something strange like that'.

Given what I've experienced, and I used to be a lot more sceptical than I am nowadays, I would like to point out that it's not 'superstititon' or 'mental illness' to believe in the existence of spirits, already I have given you several examples where I have had contact with spirits, and I was not harmed or 'possessed' like you might see in The Exorcist. I feel horror movies contribute to a negative association that a 'spirit' tends to be 'evil' and it's not how cultures like the Native Americans understand it.

I remember an interesting ESP thing with my Wii console – after starting it up and installing an update, I went to the Shop Channel and there was a 'Facebook Friend' type thing on the shop channel with some stranger I didn't know called 'Cosmos', who seemed to be modelled after the Cosmos from the Final Fantasy Dissidia games. I don't remember ever contacting this 'Cosmos' to ask her to be a 'friend' for one thing, and didn't remember there ever being a 'Facebook Friend' type system in place with the Wii.

As though this wasn't strange enough, when I checked the Virtual Console, there were far more games than usual – the Virtual Console seemed to have the entire library of games from each of the consoles on there, or at least what seemed like games that were exclusive to the Japanese Shop Channel, and I had never changed the Wii's region settings at all. There seemed to be games such as Final Fantasy III (the one remade for DS) which was exclusive to the Japanese Shop Channel, and many other games that I don't remember ever seeing on the PAL version of the Shop Channel.

Yes, you're probably thinking this sounds 'cool', but don't get too excited – after my experience, I could find no evidence of the 'Cosmos Facebook Friend on the Shop Channel' or the much larger library of games than was normally on there.

I had another interesting 'electronic ESP' during manic – but the reference will be very obscure. I was playing a game called Final Fantasy Tactics Advance, which has a 'Law' system that rewards or prohibits certain actions with either points and penalty, and there was a new 'Law Level 0' on my save file that was not there before. When I started up the save, I had access to options that were previously unavailable. I do remember some time in 2010, I think, asking a person on youtube if it was possible to mod the game to add a cleric class that had the ability to modify laws (which otherwise could only be done with cards that you had a limited quantity of), and that seems to fit with this case of ESP. Again, after my 'experience', I tried starting the game up again and found no evidence of this mod. I know it was ESP because I saw tiny specks of blue and white energy in the air –at the time this was happening -'hovering' in the middle of otherwise 'empty space', which I don't see normally.

By now, this is probably sounding very 'mystique' (mystical) to you, but letting 'strange things' mystify you (and INXS *did* sing about that) and trying to deny them rather than trying to see them as an opportunity to gain an insight into a 'spiritual reality' normally hidden from us seems counter-intuitive. Even using the words 'spiritual reality' would set some skeptics in a spin. How I look at it is, if you have 'out of this world' experiences, wouldn't you rather write it in your notebook/diary/word document hidden on your computer in a place no one but you and maybe God knows exists, rather than take an atheistic approach which offers no sense of wonder or hope?

Atheists say they want 'evidence', but what 'evidence' are they really looking for? They exist, have a brain (or not, depending who you ask), have opposable thumbs, technology that even two or three decades ago would have been thought impossible, wonders like electricity, but they argue they're 'not convinced' in the existence of God. How can you find 'evidence' if you don't even know what you're looking for? Where are they looking in the first place?

I remember starting to develop an interest, which started in late 2010 from memory, in more obscure aspects of Norse mythology, such as Njordr and the Vanir (mentioned in the Prose and Poetic Eddas, which I haven't read), and at one point I said something like 'get out of the van', and I heard the female voice from earlier say 'they wouldn't have understood it that way back then'. I interpreted this to mean that I was saying 'van' in the sense of a vehicle, like a delivery van for example, and I was being told that in ancient times, the Vikings would have understood the word 'van' as short for 'Vanir'. Why this came up, I'm not sure, but it's an interesting example how some words had very different meanings in ancient times - like the meaning of a forum in the Roman sense compared to an internet forum in modern times.

I had a slight interest (with an incredibly low interest rate that I just had to 'lock in' so I could save!) in Norse mythology before this, but I've been noticing certain elements of Norse mythology 'resonate' with me in a way that's not easy to explain. I had another situation in a Theta Healing appointment (no, that's not Scientology 'thetans' – for one thing it's much cheaper than any of that Scientology stuff, and secondly, it actually works! The name is where the similarities end!) where the words 'pissing pole' came up which afterwards I noticed was unusually similar to stanza 34 of Lokasenna (a Norse poem) – "the daughters of Hymir used you as a pisspot, and pissed in your mouth" – similar enough that I felt it couldn't be coincidence.

At one point I felt like I had horns, but I wasn't sure in what kind of way. It could have been demon horns, a samurai helmet, or a viking helmet and I don't know which one it was. It felt closer to demon horns though, and no, I wasn't 'horny', but it did feel like I had a pair of demon horns. I don't mean to say that I'm a 'demon in disguise', I hadn't literally 'grown' horns but it felt like I could feel the energy of a pair of horns at spots on the forehead where a humanoid demon would have horns. It was un sentiment étrange ('a strange feeling') and it's not one I found to be particularly comfortable. It's bad enough when there are demons on the *inside*, if you started to look like one you'd be feeling like un démon dans un monde d'hommes ('a demon in a world of men') – some might even ask what the difference between a demon and a man is !

I felt I was a demon that was rampaging and trying to 'pull up roots' so that it could sever them, the roots being less like a tree and more like telephone lines and electrical cables. To me, it felt like this 'demon' was pulling up the 'roots' (connections) of corrupt people and trying to cut them off from their power base. It was not an evil demon in the sense of wanting to hurt or kill people, but it *was* performing a task that could easily be misinterpreted as having evil intent.

There was one point where it felt like I could see in my mind a tree with twisted roots, and poison was dripping into an underground water source. I interpreted the tree as being the 'world tree' (such as the one in Norse mythology called Yggdrasil), but I wasn't sure what the significance of the twisted roots and 'poison dripping into water' represented – whether this was a real tree that had been poisoned, or whether maybe it was symbolic of the damage humanity has done to the environment. I favour a more symbolic interpretation, because it's layered (like an onion) and has a deeper meaning.

For example, this image of the tree, because of the World Tree imagery, could represent the world itself being or having become corrupt – the 'twisted roots' representing the corruption in the world and the poison, coming from the tree and entering the water, symbolising human society becoming 'poisoned' and because of the damage being done to the environment, the 'water' (not necessarily drinking water, but in a symbolic sense as representing the things necessary for life) becomes toxic and the world starts to decay instead of giving life. They'd better have top quality fertiliser if they want to give nature a jumpstart! If they used the excrement coming out of their behind instead of the excrement coming out of their mouth, we could do a lot more to 'save the planet', instead of, you know, saying 'we'll save the planet one of these days' and never getting around to it.

Bear with me if you're thinking this is becoming Norse mythology heavy, because there was plus la mythologie nordique ('more Norse mythology' – so glad I wrote it in French). At one point I was speaking what seemed like Middle Earth languages, but it was a struggle to speak.

I had an affliction called aphonia – an inability to speak. As my mind was 'crystallising', I tried to open my mouth to speak but was physically unable to. I could hear a song in my head which I don't think was an actual song, and I later wrote a song that was as close to this song I heard as I could get.

As I was struggling to speak, words that sounded like they were from Middle Earth languages started to come out of my mouth, and I barely understood what I was saying. Eventually I started making what seemed like random sounds, and started to speak the word 'ginnungagap' in slow syllables with long pauses. Ginnungagap also comes from Norse mythology, and has some similarities to the Big Bang Theory and seems to be very similar to Genesis 1:2 from the Bible – "And the earth was without form, and void; and darkness was upon the face of the deep".

While I was in my 'aphonic' state, it felt like I was trying to 'translate the gods', who knew or spoke languages so ancient that it was difficult for them to communicate in a modern language like English. I interpreted the aphonia as being my 'translation software' trying to figure out how to translate languages possibly spoken by 'gods', languages that may be so ancient that even if they were once spoken by people, may not have been spoken for hundreds of years or more. Is this proof that an extinct language never disappears completely? Maybe, maybe not. If 'gods' *were* trying to speak with me, they could have at least asked a 'god of language' to translate for them – gods *should* be able to afford a good translator, if they even need money to begin with. For some reason, even with all the things I've mentioned about Norse mythology, it seemed like it was the *Greek* gods trying to communicate with me ('all Greek to me' after all!) – I sensed a bearded, very Zeus-like figure and was convinced it was an acceptable interpretation. Although, the figure of Zeus has a few image problems - a promiscuous 'king of the gods' doesn't exactly make for a positive role model, so maybe it's time for some *re*-interpretation.

There seemed to be a stone statue, or what looked like a statue of the Roman god Janus that suddenly came to life. The statue seemed like it was Janus sleeping, and when he awoke, his 'consciousness' for lack of a better word flew outwards in the cardinal (not bishop!) directions. I remember having what seemed like visions of a 'Trials of Janus' that had something to do with a 'shortening of the days' – that time was once chaotic and long periods of time passed with very little happening, and the 'length of the days' was measured according to 'the gods', because there were no humans on Earth to measure time (prehistoric Earth).

Once these trials had 'caught up' with the modern world, the concept of time became 'standardised' and questions like 'what can be achieved in just one day?' took on a modern context. It was as though 'le monde antique avait à rattraper le monde moderne' ('the ancient world had to catch up to the modern world'), but that the modern world also needed to rediscover some aspects of the ancient world. There's 'ancient history', and there's 'ancient *wisdom*' – which one do you think is relevant to the modern world ?

This 'standardisation of time' seemed to be known as the 'shortening of the days' and was an unusual phenomenon because (in human history) so much progress was acheived (e.g technologically, scientifically) in such a short space of time that the ancient world needed to 'catch up', or depending how you look at it, the 'ancestors' or, if you believe in reincarnation, the modern 'incarnations' of the people from the ancient world had to learn many new things in a very short space of time. Due to modern technology, time would be literally 'shortened' to hours and minutes instead of days or weeks in some cases, and even though technology made people lives much easier, they were *less* happy and *less* satisfied.

It was as though 'the ancients' (and hopefully not the ones from Stargate who Daniel Jackson thought 'didn't do much of anything') were less primitive than we believed them to be, because we were looking at our modern technology and had developed a 'technological arrogance', that in *some* ways our modern world is worse than the ancient world – global warming (I dare you to say global warming was worse in the ancient world! The concept of 'carbon emissions' didn't even exist!), the worst wars in human history, greed to an extent that would have been unimaginable in the ancient world...What I'm trying to say is, are we really as 'developed' as some countries believe themselves to be ?

I remember there being an 'East versus West' type of scenario where The West was highly advanced technologically and 'economically' but the East while the East was considered 'underdeveloped' technologically, it was overall more advanced because of its spirituality, and the West was being put in an 'evolve or die' scenario where it had to catch up to The East or risk its entire civilisation collapse. This seemed to take the form of a vision, where there were images of many Hindu deities and a few images of deities from the West, such as the Norse deities, but they appeared saddened or disappointed because the West was in a spiritually underdeveloped state, and the Western deities felt the West had turned their back on them. They were not looking for 'la religion' (to be 'worshipped'), they were looking for vénération (I don't need to translate this one, do I ?) – to be respected and to help humanity realise its mistakes. It gave me an impression of 'the gods' felt a sense of pity for Man, because Man was following a materialistic path and in the West, the 'gods' 'ne figurait pas dans leur philosophie' ('didn't figure into their philosophy').

There was a strong sense of hope from this, because the 'gods', or at least the ones I had visions of were not warlike or tyrannical by any means, but were fairly humble and felt genuine sorrow for humanity. They were sidéré ('dumbstruck') that humanity would try to diminish the value of spirituality with science and put a higher value on money than friendships, family, or honour. The general feeling was, if you've seen the

Marvel 'Thor' movies, imagining Odin shaking his head and saying 'when will they learn ?'

I remember performing what seemed vaguely like magic – what I named 'stitching time' where I would send healing to a particular time and place and it was as though that time and place was loose thread that was being restitched. I've heard the expression 'a stitch in time saves nine', but it felt like this was some kind of 'mental direction' where I was directing these 'stitches' to particular places at particular times.

It felt as though eventually the 'needle' developed into a bow that could shoot an arrow through time, that the needle had become 'self-aware' in some sense because of what I was doing.

These stitches weren't literal stitches like in sewing, it seemed more like healing of traumatic events, where the stitches needed to be sent to a specific place or specific people. This was the first time I saw things in terms of a needle – 'sewing the seams' of 'torn lives', before this I tended to think of the world in terms of separation such as language, culture etc but I was beginning to see the world as more interconnected – if a person in one country prayed, a country on the other side of the world might be healed. The healing would have a limited effect, but would be in a better condition than before the prayer.

Imagine the possibilties (and all the people) who could benefit from an insight like this ! If we fail to accept this as a possibility, the possibility that we may actually have the ability to heal the world ! At least one person must have already realised this, because he wrote a song about it. Now I wonder, who could have written a song about 'healing the world'. I've given you a clue, but I don't want to spoil it.

Once while I was at a shopping centre, I sat down and then started seeing bugs crawling over the entire floor. These weren't ordinary flies, but bugs about the size of a tennis ball and the entire floor was covered. I closed my eyes, and as soon as I opened them again, the bugs were gone. I remember hearing something telepathically afterwards, about Beelzebub 'taking a dump', and interpreted it to mean Beelzebub (whoever *he* is – not a name that would go far in marketing) was 'dumping his negativity' in the form of these bugs - taking a dump in the sense of a toilet – that he was expelling negativity he didn't need any more (and probably didn't sign for either – stuff that was probably 'dumped on him' without a return address) and those bugs, which appeared to be made of spiritual energy was a discharge of that energy. I say 'spiritual energy' because they had a golden brown appearance and disappeared as soon as I closed and opened my eyes again, and no one else appeared to have seen them.

Sounds like something from a horror movie, right ? But this was no movie – it would've been an incredibly short one if it was. What I interpreted the bugs to mean is that 'Beelzebub' was dumping the negativity associated with him that he didn't want (and wasn't able to Return to Sender) – such as the name 'Lord of Flies' and the imagery associated with that name – a gigantic 'demon fly', that made him think 'how do I *not* be *that* guy ?'.

Who Beelzebub really is is something that not many people have wondered, but the name is so notorious that there is a bat called the Beelzebub Bat, and a toad called Beelzebufo named after him, so I can understand why he wouldn't want that kind of publicity. I believe the name 'Beelzebub' is a mistranslation from Hebrew of either Baal Zephon or Baal Hadad, and I think of it in terms of it being used as an insult, and being equivalent to calling Baal Hadad 'a zebu', but that the name stuck, and well, the rest is history…and in the case of Beelzebufo, fairly recent history.

One 'event', if you don't mind me calling it that that I remember fondly was a spirit visitation. There were four spirits who visited me – I couldn't see them with my eyes, I was seeing them mentally. If you remember, I mentioned spirit visitation before, but there was no way this was a person mistaken for a spirit.

'Spirit' sounds better in French, so if you don't mind I'll call them 'esprit'. Hopefully about now, if you're cluey, you remember I mentioned Native Americans and 'the spirits'. If you don't know what a spirit is, they are a being of spiritual energy and even a femme séduisante (an 'attractive woman') has only a fraction of the beauty that these 'beings' (who are definitely not the 'human' type of being !) have.

From what I've seen, esprit are luminescent and radiate spiritual energy and light. There *are* stories of encounters of the (whatever number of 'kind' of encounter with a spirit counts as) have come into contact with a demonic entity, but this is not that kind of story. If it's from a horror movie, then I don't even *watch* that kind of story !

These four spirits were all female and very 'séduisant' and if I remember correctly, they were all blonde. They were all dressed in white dresses, which gave them a 'vibe' of purity. None of them showed anything but gentleness towards me, and I felt a strong 'sacred feminine' vibe from them. I couldn't tell you what 'world' they were from, only that wherever 'there' is, it's out of this one.

From what I've seen so far, masculine-looking espirt and feminine esprit (definitely not ghosts!) aren't very different in appearance – the masculine-looking esprit have a different hairstyle and broader shoulders and upper body, but are much more attractive than the average man. Masculine esprit (such as the 'beautiful spirit' I mentioned from '06) seem to have 'mastered' the look of bishonen – their facial features seem more gentle and more feminine than a human male, but they're still in some ways more attractive than a human female due to their spiritual 'radiance'.

There was nothing 'mean-spirited' about these four 'esprit' – all four of them had a gentle presence and there was no hostility or 'mauvaise volonté' (ill will) towards me at all.

None of them spoke and I had no idea what any of their names were, but I remember them wrapping a white cloth around my waist, then leaving. I would've liked to have known their names, but my 'headspace' at the time was that I could only see them mentally because what I had then was a failure to communicate.

I haven't seen them again since, but I would like to learn their names – any positive spiritual encounters (in other words, anything that doesn't have a horror movie vibe), I see as a possibilité d'apprendre ('opportunity to learn'). Very few people have this kind of 'spiritual connection', but if more people did, there'd be a lot fewer people like Dawkins in the world. Quite frankly, just one of him is more than enough !

 Now we come to one of the highlights of '2011 Manic', which is a pretty uninspired name. How about we call it 'l'expérience 2011' ?

Almost everyone will have at least heard of a mysterious figure called 'Jesus' – I'd ask you to raise your hand if you've heard of him, but this is a book, not a seminar, so I can't count the hands you're using to hold this book because I have no idea what position they're in and maybe I don't want to know. If this was a seminar, I'd have also asked you to raise your hand if you've been in contact with Jesus.

Having trouble following ? Personally, I don't consider myself a follower of Jesus but after the experience I'm about to describe, I'm willing to listen to his paroles de sagesse ('words of wisdom') any time.

While manic, there was a point where I took out a Bible, hoping I would find something to reassure me. What I found was amazing ! There was strong ESP – I was seeing all kinds of energy, and as I was reading the Bible, there seemed to be writing that was addressed to me, as though Jesus was writing to me specifically. This was a profound time – this wasn't about 'finding Jesus', this was Jesus finding *me*. There were pages and pages of messages written to me, but I've only be sharing what I remember.

"Moses must not cross the Jordan" – this struck me as unusual, why would Jesus be saying Moses not be allowed to 'cross the Jordan'. It's possible that 'cross the Jordan' is some kind of expression with a different meaning, but I interpret it literally as referring to the Jordan river.

Why he would be forbidden from crossing the Jordan, I'm not sure. This seemed to me like some kind of alternate reality or time travel, where 'they' (Jesus and the ones working with him) were actively trying to prevent him from crossing that river. My theories range from being so that Moses couldn't spread the Ten Commandments to preventing Moses from achieving some other goal that Jesus and the spirits realised had made things worse and they felt they had to prevent it from having happened. Keep in mind this is how I interpreted it after the experience, at the time I was overwhelmed mentally by everything that was happening.

"The Days Are Evil" – I interpreted this to have a fairly obvious meaning of 'the times are dark' or 'these are hard times to be in', that the times we live in now are difficult times because of what is being done to the Earth for the sake of progress and 'economic growth', and that Jesus was expressing his disapproval of the current worldview.

'I've been shipwrecked three times' (there was also mention of muggings and robbery) – I was unsure how to interpret this, because of the mention of muggings and robbery, I believed it was describing things that happened in Jesus' lifetime, but the mention of being 'shipwrecked' seemed like an expression. It sounded as though he was describing having been 'stranded' or 'in a situation there was no way out of' three times and he was telling me this because he saw a kindred spirit in me.

"Where did you first hear about my crucifixion?" – I wasn't sure why he was asking this, and the way he asked this question made it sound as though he was surprised in some way. Was he expressing surprise that his crucifixion had taken on religious elements? Or was he making some kind of broader statement about Christianity? I leave this one open to interpretation, see what you can make of it.

'Faith to speak' – This sounded like he was talking about someone who felt they couldn't speak their mind because they were afraid of being judged or criticised, so they stayed silent to avoid 'upsetting' other people. I interpreted this as Jesus saying that it's acceptable to have the faith to speak your mind even if other people don't agree with it. This has profound meaning for anyone who ever felt they were being silenced.

"We will not be made slaves to Elemental Lords" – I interpreted this as referencing my creative writing, where he was pointing out that we are not slaves to 'gods of the elements'. He must have felt I needed to be told this or I would be treating my writing as 'real' and not treating it as fictional.

"We will not be made slaves to the Lord of Impure Air" – This seemed fairly obvious, he was talking about Baal Hadad, whose more commonly known name 'Beelzebub' may translate as 'Lord of Impure Air', and we don't have to be made slaves to a 'god of the elements'.

"Blessings first on the Gentiles" – I'm not sure what sort of blessings this was referring to, but it's the opposite on the belief of 'blessings first on the Jews', which implies either non-Jewish people are receiving more blessings, or that the 'Gentiles' need certain blessings more urgently and that the Jews will receive extra because of having to wait.

"We found incredible ignorance in Asia" – This is another one I wasn't sure about. He mentioned 'in Asia', but there was no mention of where or when. He may have meant ancient times, or he may have been referring to the modern world. There wasn't enough information to go on.

"I am debating whether or not to come down and visit you" – This one was incredible for a few reasons. First, Jesus is suggesting that he's interested in coming to visit me personally, which for many people would be a great honour. Second, it gives further evidence that there must be somewhere to 'come down' *from* if he is communicating through the Bible and suggesting this possibility in the first place.

"A Man still sleeps with his Father's Wife" – I was unsure of the meaning of this one as well. It may have been a parable, or an unfamiliar expression, because taken literally it would be saying a 'man' was having an affair with his 'father's wife'. There may have been an entirely different meaning, but this one was lost on me.

"We know what the Enemy is up to" – Another fairly obvious one, referring to the Devil or evil spirits in general. The fact that he said 'we know *what* they're up to' should be reassuring for anyone who is afraid of evil spirits.

"The Son approached The Father of his own accord" – This is interesting, because while Jesus is referred to as 'The Son' in Christianity, here Jesus is talking in the third person, where it sounds like he's not talking about himself, but possibly someone else who is known as 'The Son'. Again, not enough information to go on, and there may have been more 'Jesus writings', but I don't remember in enough detail.

So what do you think, is this 'happening' enough for you? I've come to the end of describing my 2006, 2008 and 2011 experiences, but there is still more for you to sink your teeth into, and if you're needing to 'sink your teeth', maybe you should have something to eat, or go brush your teeth *in* the sink.

I hope you feel like you're getting your money's worth from this book, keep reading, and maybe someday someone will be lucky enough to pick this book up from a secondhand shop for dirt cheap – anything under $5 is a steal!

ESP, Yes Please

By now you might be starting to think I've 'seen it all', but I'm starting to feel that what I've seen so far is the tip of the iceberg and it seems like I'm only scratching the surface, or I'd have come up with a better expression.

This chapter will be about examples of ESP that I've experienced, as well as a mini-manic in 2015. The experiences I've described already have convinced me not only that there is plus de ce monde ('more than this world'), but also given me glimpses of 'life on the other side'.

But the manic 'experiences' I've described so far are just the most intense ESP I've experienced, I've had other ESP experiences outside of a 'manic experience' and for your education (I was going to say 'entertainment', unless you find reading a book *that* fun) I'm sharing some other ESP experiences.

One example of ESP I've experienced a lot is a mysterious breeze in the middle of the room. Usually this happens while sitting on the toilet. You might be thinking I just left the air conditioner on and forgot about it. Well, the 'spooky' thing about this breeze is that I could be sitting on the toilet with the door closed, window locked and no air conditioner on, and this strange breeze would blow through the middle of the room and unlike wind, I could almost see it.

This has happened more than once, and I even saw an actor being interviewed on TV say that this had happened to them. Even for a skeptic, if several people report the same thing, it's much harder to dismiss it and not for manque de preuves ('lack of evidence').

If you believe people who hear voices are crazy, you might want to skip this next part. Remember that female voice I mentioned before? I've heard that voice *many* times and 'she' (assuming she's a spirit) has always been full of encouragement – one time she called me 'an amazing writer', and I was so relieved that someone had recognised me as a writer. This voice has almost never been insulting, bossy or threatening in any way, apart from one time she told me to shut up because I was thinking too much about a particular subject and was being too negative.

I don't know who this 'voice' is, but if she's a spirit, her voice is very similar to the girl I mentioned who I said I'd learned Gratitude, Forgiveness and Unconditional Love from. Her voice is very similar. Whoever she is, she's very kind hearted and one time told me that she loves me, so when I hear her voice, I usually take notice of what she's saying.

If you're a skeptic, you probably find the idea of 'talking to spirits' to be a ridiculous concept, but is it really safe to assume anyone that hears voices at all is mentally ill by default rather than being open to the idea that these people may be psychically 'in tune'? That's of course assuming you believe in anything psychic, but isn't even the possibility that they may be communicating with an otherworldly 'being' something significant enough to worth being open to?

I'm not exaggerating when I say this 'spirit' has had a profound effect on me – she has given me reassurance on so many occasions that I may be less of a man than I am now without her kind words. Whoever she is, she is not some horror movie character – she has never tried to hurt me, has never told *me* to hurt anyone or to do anything destructive. I have a sense of déjà vu (this one loses something in translation) with this spirit, I can't see her but I know she's there, somewhere 'watching over me' as they say. Hopefully she has something else to watch during the 'boring moments' of my life, because some moments of my life are so boring that I'd change the channel, if there was a channel to change in the first place.

From time to time, I have ESP moments where I see flashes of energy. Generally these flashes of energy are like tiny wisps, vaguely resembling pyreflies and the Farplane from Final Fantasy X. If you're unfamiliar with the Final Fantasy series, just Google 'pyreflies' to get an idea what I'm talking about. Why is that starting to sound like a black character from a sitcom saying 'know what I'm talkin' 'bout?'

There's a huge difference between what I see with ESP and 'pyreflies' though, and that's the appearance. The size of the flashes I see are usually small flecks maybe the size of a fingernail, which appear in the middle of 'empty space'. One time I was meditating and I saw a large number of gold flecks, which is unusual because normally they're blue, white, or a bluish white, sometimes red, sometimes yellow, and a fair amount of the time they're a kind of pinkish colour.

These flecks are a sign that through meditation, chanting mantras and generally being open minded, 'evidence' of 'other worlds' will be revealed to you, and the more open you are, the more often these unexplained events will happen.

As if all I've described so far wasn't enough, one time I had written something about the Dark Ages and I began seeing ESP of red and yellow 'clumps' (not flecks - much bigger and much 'dirtier' looking), which at the time I thought 'okay, that's a bit strange', but later I was walking home from the shops one time and I heard the line 'We don't need no thought control' from Another Brick in the Wall seemingly out of nowhere. I sometimes hear songs, or certain lines from specific songs, but this was what I call 'spooky'.

I don't have Another Brick in the Wall on iTunes, or even have any Pink Floyd albums, but I heard a specific line from that song as though 'the universe' knew the exact song that 'resonated' with how I was feeling and what I was thinking. Starting to sound too mystical? So does a lot of the material on spirituality that's out there! For example, 'the spiritual is within and without', 'the spiritual is everywhere and nowhere' – it's very helpful if you grasp the meaning, but that's exactly the kind of talk that puts so many people off of spirituality.

I'm not going to try to convince you of 'otherworldly contact' or any of the obscure things associated with the term 'New Age', but I feel that thoughts are like a radio – they can be tuned into the right 'frequency' for ESP, or they can be tuned in the opposite direction to a lower frequency. Frequency, besides being a movie, is a scientific concept, so not everything spiritual necessarily has to be separate from science.

I also remind there being a strange smell for a good part of 2014, it seemed to be everywhere I went, which led me to believe it was 'bad vibes' that were going around during 2014 that I was smelling. The idea of smelling bad vibes may sound ridiculous to some of you, but if you remember the Beach Boys song Good Vibrations, the story behind the song was about dogs barking at bad energy, which they're apparently a lot better at picking up because they have a much stronger sense of smell.

What exactly do I mean by 'bad vibes'? Well, even if you don't believe in the concept of 'vibration', have you ever noticed certain situations or certain people that gave you a bad feeling and you had to get yourself out of those situations or away from those people as quickly as you could? Some might call it intuition, but a strange group of people called 'atheists' might dismiss that idea. I don't mind them, because if you separate the 'a' from the 'theist' part, they become 'a theist'.

What was it about 2014 that gave it a feeling of 'bad vibes'? My theory is that because there were a lot of documentaries about World War I linked to the 100th

anniversary, there were lingering emotions from World War I that were being brought to the surface by everything that was being done for the 100th anniversary. In some of the documentaries I saw, there was a general feeling that the war was pointless and anger at the politicians that were responsible for the war.

Even though this could be seen as good, a chance to heal and move on, there seemed to be a deep sense of regret related to the war and this could have been responsible for the 'bad vibes' I was smelling. There seemed to be a musty smell everywhere I went that had a feeling of 'being stuck in the past', like the feeling of seeing old 1800's or early 1900's photos where the photos are all in sepia tone and have an 'old world' feel about them compared to modern photos. Given the choice of vieux monde ('old world') or nouveau monde ('new world'), nouveau monde wins every time.

Back to what I was saying about having 'written something about the Dark Ages', for a moment, I heard 'chatter' while I was sleeping one time (well, probably *more* than one time, but I don't need to tell you that !) related to witches.

I heard a man say, 'How dare they ! The audacity !'

Then I heard another voice say, 'How dare *they* make such accusations !'

Another voice then said, 'That is not love ! That is not mercy ! That is not forgiveness !'

The same voice continued on to say, 'These deeds have gone down in history !'

Then, 'Beyond monstrous'

Then, 'Look what you have done !'

Then, 'On your knees, beg for forgiveness'

Then something where I can't remember the full wording, but something about mentioning the word 'Devil' too much, and 'continues to this day'.

Then the voice continued with, '(creative) works are (currently) insufficient. More must be done'

Besides writing it all down, I did nothing else about this 'Witch Dialogue' as I've called it. After all, this was just 'more ESP' to me, which is why it belongs in this book.

I *did* have one other manic 'experience', but this one was more of a 'mini' manic, it was far less intense than the previous ones. It started in early June, instead of 'Mad March' like has happened with 'manic' in the past.

At first I didn't notice anything hors de l'ordinaire ('out of the ordinary'), but eventually my thoughts became dominated by Nazi Germany and I started feeling shame at being half-German. I find it easier to just laugh at this person called 'Hitler' – I remember making jokes about Hitler having 'taken a few **hits** in the sanity department' and linking 'sanity' with Sanity music, imagining if Hitler was in a Sanity music store. I also remember imagining what it would be like if Hitler had to see a psychiatrist, and heard a different female voice to the usual one say 'he probably wouldn't even go'. One thing's for sure, he was definitely a git, so maybe it's better to call him 'Gitler' for a laugh or two.

I could probably think of a few other names for him if you gave me enough time, but we'll settle with 'git'. At least one of them is one you don't want to mention in polite company.

On 7/6/15, while I was walking near the shops, I remember believing that I was 'Legion'. Legion was a demon in the Bible who was reputed to have been exorcised (that's exorcise with an 'o', now the other kind of exercise, which unless you're a health nut *makes* you say 'oh, do I have to ?') who was made notoriously infamous by the quote 'I am Legion, for We Are Many'. I began to believe that I was the 'real' Legion, and was overcome by grief and actually crying on that day.

The grief having this belief caused me is hard to describe. I began to believe that I was a demon and that Legion was a way of disguising my identity. If you asked me now if I believe I'm Legion, I'd say definitely not, but you have to keep in mind that while manic you can't control your thoughts, and sometimes can't control your mouth either.

I was believing that whoever 'Legion' was, I was him, and there was incessant 'l'esper-ience' (ESP – telepathy especially) for much of that day until I returned home. This was one of the earliest signs I remember of being 'manic', and it distressed me enough that if a person had walked past me while I was walking along, they would have thought something was wrong.

Even though this was an early warning sign, I tried to pay as little attention to it as I could hoping my mental state would improve on its own, but manic was already setting in.

On 8/6/15 – I heard 'ESP music' that seemed to come from nowhere. It sounded as though it was coming from above me, and I saw an image above me of a fairy playing a violin. I believe I've had contact with this fairy before, the name 'Anla' keeps coming up, but until this point I had never seen her.

This fairy seemed to be trying to relax me by playing this music, and even though it helped, it wasn't enough to arrêter le maniaque dans sa voie ('stop the manic in its tracks'). Whoever she is or was, she seemed to be a very gentle fairy and there seemed to be something familiar about her.

This was the first time I remember hearing music through ESP, but I (not so secretly) hope that it won't be the last. Hearing the music gave me the focus (was it a Ford ?) to do what I felt I needed to do to get through the rest of the 'experience'.

In case you're wondering, the music sounded much sharper than on ordinary violin, probably because a fairy counts as a spirit, so it would be a much sharper frequency.

This 'mini-manic' seemed to centre heavily on the Nazis, and I felt overwhelming shame at being half-German. In my mind I made a list of things I liked about Germany and a list of things I didn't like, and on computer I wrote 'Ja' for each thing that I liked. For example, I wrote 'ja' for schnitzel, 'ja' for strudel, 'ja' for Einstein, 'nein' for German beer especially because of the word stein for a beer mug and I made the connection of 'fill a stein' with 'Philistine' (i.e I imagined Germany as being the Philistines because of the Nazis). I was also making connection with the word German, e.g 'germ warfare' – 'german warfare', 'german – germ man'. Even the word 'manic' became part of this – the word Germanic literally became Ger*manic*.

The female voice I heard that was different to the usual one I believed belonged to a German exchange student I had met at high school. There had been an incident where, being in the bad headspace I was in during 2006, I asked her for a hug and she became upset. Looking at it now, I wasn't looking for a relationship with her, because I was told she already had a boyfriend, I was connecting with her because, being half-German, I sympathised with her situation and I was reaching out to her to say 'it's alright'. I didn't see it that way at the time, but with the benefit of hindsight I feel sympathy for having come from a country with such a traumatic history.

I felt an overwhelming sense of guilt for having hurt her which I hadn't been feeling or hadn't realise until this mini-manic came along. I recognised that her surname had links to the Nazis and became obsessed with something I was calling 'spiritual rebirthing' – I felt I had a duty to sever her links to the 'old' Germany. Being half-German, it felt as though I had a duty to the German people.

I began looking through various dictionaries – German, Icelandic, Danish trying to find a new surname for her that sever the Nazi connection. It was slow going at first, and I was beginning to become more and more manic, until I looked in the Danish dictionary and found the word 'helgessen' ('saintly') and decided it was perfect. I considered using the Danish dictionary because in my mind I made a connection of Danish = 'Dan-ish', and because when I think of the word 'Danish', the edible kind of Danish comes to mind. Just don't try 'eating a danish' in Denmark unless you're in a bakery – they probably won't take kindly to cannabalism!

I had an image in my head of her moving to Iceland and learning to speak Icelandic, followed by an idea of Hitler being taken to a mental hospital in Iceland, where he would spend all day talking about what food he likes on Twitter and no one online paying any attention, and the doctors would discuss his 'progress' (which there was a continual lack of).

Some numerology began to come through, which I assumed came from Metatron, because I there was a time where I stayed up all night typing on computer, and felt like information was coming through ESP. The following 'proclamation' I believed came through Metatron, '6/6/2006 – The Fuhrer of Lies has fallen and shall rise no more', as well as something I believed came from some 'New Age Gospels', 'A 'New Age' Fuhrer shall rise from the South'.

The 6/6/2006 is significant because of the three '6's, which I interpreted as meaning that as of 6/6/2006, everything related to Hitler had been 'balanced out' and he would never again be able to rise to power (such as through reincarnation). The three 6's also represented the number 666, because I got the impression that Hitler was either the Antichrist (now there's a word with a lot of baggage! Where do I check out?) or was believed to have been. Also, 6/6 is the birthday of the exchange student, which is unusual because (in 2006) I remember asking her when her birthday was and at the time having no idea why.

The 'New Age Gospels' I believed were to be 'communicated' through Metatron and supervised by Jesus, where it was like a 'Good News Bible' modern interpretation of the Book of Revelation that took away the prophecies of doom and gloom and focused on the 'Good News', and would be revealed gradually on the internet with daily 'proclamations' either from Jesus or with a Popular Culture reference. A sort of 'évangile selon à Jesus', ('Gospel according *to* Jesus') rather than a 'Évangile de Jésus' ('gospel *about* Jesus').

I remember looking at a particular website about Metatron and feeling 'lit up' mentally, performing a meditation on Canaanite and Sumerian religion and having ideas about 'sacred sex' and sacredness as part of something called the 'Anu Code'.

There was a mysterious door knock at one point, and when I went to answer the door, I looked through the peephole and saw someone, or something in the shape of a person made of wispy energy, just like the 'flecks' (appearing as though they were made entirely out of pyreflies), and when I opened the door, they disappeared completely, without saying anything.

You might think it's strange I can talk about this so calmly, but this is not the first time this 'coup de porte mystérieuse' ('mysterious door knock') has happened. By my count it's happened three times. This time the 'fantôme' (ghost) or 'esprit' (spirit) was female, and was female the time before that, but the first time this 'mysterious door knock phenomenon' happened, the 'spirit' was male and dressed in a white formal shirt with black pants.

I've heard of spirit visitation, and this seems to explain it well, because if it was a ghost, if I could *see* it, I should have been able to talk to it, whereas it's possible a 'spirit' can visit then disappear suddenly, because they're having to lower their energy to be able to appear in a human-like form to be able to knock on a door. A ghost on the other hand would probably walk straight through the door rather than knocking first.

Don't be scared by the idea of ghosty figures knocking on your door then disappearing, it probably won't happen to you, but if it does, try asking them who they are and see what happens. There was nothing hostile or 'horror movie vibe' about it (and don't get any ideas about turning this door knock thing into a horror movie – if you enjoy horror movies for the scare factor there must be something *horror*-bly wrong with you.

Whoever these 'spirits' are, they obviously *want* to visit me, I'm not performing any rituals or contacting these spirits telepathically to make them come to me, they're coming to me de leur propre gré ('of their own free will'), but it would be nice to manage a *proper gre*eting.

If you're curious about this idea, try praying and asking for a spirit to visit you at your house and see what l'univers ('the universe') comes back with. The spirit might have had to travel *across* the universe if they've been busy, but try it before you knock it – you might be surprised by the results.

Around the 15th of June, I remember the strangest sensation. After coming home from the doctor, crying the whole time because of the shame and guilt I mentioned, everything seemed different. On the way home, it seemed much darker outside than usual. Even with street lights on, the air seemed to have some kind of mystérieux ('mysterious') energy about it that it doesn't usually have. It wasn't because 'love' was in the air, either.

 It seemed as though there was some kind of energy hovering in the air that isn't usually there, or if it is, I'm normally unaware of. The best way I can think to describe it as is fumé miroir de salle de bains ('smoky bathroom mirror') – normally the air seems more 'clear' at night, but on this particular night there was some kind of haze.

I had a theory about it being connected to the moon in some way, and called it 'heavy moon dust', because it felt like it was some kind of energy given off by the moon. Since I'm a Cancerian, the star sign whose planet is the moon, this would make sense. If there was any disturbance with the moon, I'd more more likely to sense it than other star signs because Cancer is more sensitive to the moon. I may not be the homme dans la lune ('man in the moon'), but sometimes it feels like I'm the homme *de* la lune ('man *from* the moon').

It's actually unfair being Cancer in some ways – a lot of diseases are named after your star sign (e.g skin cancer, lung cancer), and your sign's planet, the moon is the source of a lot of ancient superstition. For example, the moon is associated with stories of werewolves, the word 'lunatic' (which has a strong link with mental hospitals), even worse the word 'loony', as in 'loony bin'

This 'l'énergie de la lune lourde' ('heavy moon energy) continued into the following day (the 16th or 17th), and there was very strong telepathic communication involved. I was having a lot of trouble trying to ask 'the voices' who they were so that I could identify who I was talking to. Jesus' name came up a lot - he seemed to be correcting mistranslated or misunderstood Bible passages, for example, 'Money is the root of all evil' was 'corrected' as 'Money is the root of many injustices', and

'Blessed are the meek, for they shall inherit the earth' was 'corrected' as 'Blessed are the most humble in spirit', because the word 'meek' had been distorted and some had claimed to be meek when they were anything but. Jesus seemed to agree with a lot of what I was thinking and it felt as though I was talking to a kindred spirit.

Other times it was hard to identify who was talking. It was too difficult to keep the conversation completely in my head, so at times 'the voices' seemed like they were 'talking *through* me' because there was too much l'activité mentale ('mental activity') for me to keep asking the voices I was hearing who they were.

By the time I got back home, one thing lead to another, and an ambulance appeared to take me into hospital (again! Do I get loyalty club benefits?). As I was climbing onto the stretcher, I noticed there was a feeling of peace as I was being loaded into the ambulance, a feeling of peace I didn't have other times I was taken into hospital.

As I was waiting inside the hospital, I was still feeling grief and crying, but it felt as though the shame and guilt were 'drying up'. Throughout my hospital stay, I felt fairly in control, never felt disorientated like previous times and met some wonderful people. I even asked the nurses for extra medication any time I felt 'the voices' were becoming too 'volume élevé' ('high volume').

I only spent three weeks in hospital, the shortest of any of my hospital stays, and when I was discharged from hospital, I felt like I was 'free', like all the shame and guilt had disappeared and I was finally at peace. About a week after being discharged from hospital, I continued working on this book, and was excited to 'get back to work' because I now had more to write about – I saw this 2015 'manic experience' as a positive thing, it was only the experience of being in hospital that was negative.

If anything, I saw the 2015 'experience' as a sign that I was meant to write this book, and gained a 'nouveau sens du but' ('new sense of purpose'). My only regret is that you've almost reached the end of the book, and if you're a skeptic and I haven't helped to open your mind even a *little* by this point, then you're a hard person to convince. I've tried to explain what I've experienced as well as I can in words, but the 'spiritual' (which is the most vague and broad word I've come across and it's no wonder so many people are put off by mentioning it) must be experienced to make sense of it. That, and words have trouble describing things that other people haven't seen. 'Oh yeah, *that*', I hope you're thinking.

After reading this book, I also hope you'll be *doing* more thinking – some many people just 'act' first.

Conclusion Pour L'inclusion

As you can tell by now, it's been a journey, and so has writing this book. I hope I've given you at least *something* to ponder. If you're a skeptic and I haven't managed to convince you yet, can I suggest joining the Richard Dawkins' fanclub?

That was a joke, but this book was anything but. These 'experiences' allowed me to grow and learn, and I'm grateful that I had them, even though they were a real mal de tête ('headache'), literally.

Out of curiousity, if you're reading this and you *are* an atheist, I have a few questions for you. These questions are only to atheists (already believing in God before reading this book comes highly recommended, and if you do, then je vous remercie beaucoup d'être un croyant [Translate this one for yourself, you might be surprised]) :

- ☐ If you claim you won't believe in anything besides science unless you're presented with 'evidence', but when evidence appears that would be enough to convince many or even most people, and yet still say 'there's not enough evidence to believe in God' or something similar, then what kind of 'evidence' are you expecting to be presented with?"
- ☐ Is it acceptable to make radical atheistic claims that go against the beliefs of the majority of people and would be likely to offend many people

only because you don't believe in anything (besides science)?
- ☐ If even what I've described in this book, based on first-hand experience, is not enough to at least make you *ponder* the idea of there being something other than this world, then do you really want to spend the rest of your life believing 'death is the end'"?
- ☐ Is atheism a 'power trip' for you that allows you to ridicule what other believe and claim 'freedom of belief' as justification? Be honest!

Now that I've covered that base (which would be a lot more useful if I was playing baseball), de passer aux précroyants ('moving to the pre-believers' – that's right, I created the word '*pre*-believers' - there's no way I'd say something completely uncool like 'existing theists'), these experiences profoundly changed my life for the better.

To begin with, the phrase 'go Manic' was invented, if you consider that a good thing, and I've taken to using the phrase 'manic brilliance' (first used to describe Robin Williams' performances) as a slightly ironic way of putting a positive spin on these experiences. You've probably already noticed I've being using the phrase 'manic experience' rather than the clinical 'manic episode' because it sounds more positive and is more meaningful, an 'experience' gives more of an idea of what it was, rather than 'episode' which sounds like étiquette psychiatrique terribles ('a terrible psychiatric label'). That, and 'manic episode' sounds like an episode of a TV show called 'Manic'. Remind me to never watch *that* show!

I remember recently watching a documentary about the last days of Michael Hutchence (lead singer of INXS), and some of what it described sounded like in his final days he was going through something similar to 'manic'. I got the impression he didn't know what was happening to him, and because he didn't know what was happening, he wasn't able to get the help he needed to reste en vie ('stay alive') – maybe if someone had played the song 'Stayin' Alive', it might have helped.

Even though it sounded like he was taking drugs before he died, a lot of what the documentary described sounded very similar to 'manic', and if that was the case, then it's no surprise he couldn't handle it because his mental state was already impaired by the drugs. I point this out because this is what can happen if 'manic' gets out of hand – a person can end up dying due to drugs or from starvation.

What I believe was *his* 'manic' seemed to be more drug induced, whereas *my* 'experiences' happened suddenly, and I was only taking prescription medication. I feel a sense of empathy for what Michael Hutchence went through, but also a sense of disappointment that manic 'experiences' are so little understood par le grand public ('by the public at large'), and people who have been through them need to be treated with moins d'hostilité ('less hostility') because these people can offer unique spiritual insights. It's time we started having a mental health system that didn't *put* people through hell !

After these 'experiences', I have a much greater sense of hope. It's not just that my 'belief in God' has become stronger, I've been 'shown' (since there's 'nothing you can see that isn't shown') that things can get better, and just because they may seem 'doom and gloom', there *is* hope. Even just believing in God, even if it's not a very strong belief can give you the strength to face any obstacles. By having no sense of hope (I'm looking at you, atheists), there is no 'getting better', going to 'a better place', no 'better state of mind' – by believing 'there is no hope', you're creating that perception of 'reality' for yourself.

Logic (and some obscure branches of science) says that there must be some form of creative intelligence – how can inanimate matter randomly 'create itself out of nothing' and create life and intelligence by random processes? How can you have 'natural selection' without suggesting genes have some form of intelligence? One time, while writing this book, I saw a flash of purple energy in front of me, to the right of the computer. It's hard to doubt the existence of God, or the 'Creator', or the 'Great Spirit' or one of probably a dozen other names when things like that happen fairly regularly (but not as regular as sitting on 'the throne', but that's a different kind of 'regular').

Until I had these experiences, I wouldn't have thought of myself as spiritual. I'm not saying I was an atheist, Dieu pardonne ('God forbid'), but I would have been skeptical of anything using the word 'spiritual' – there were some things I definitely believed almost all along, but other things I've opened up to since having these weird but wonderful experiences.

I continue to have ESP on a regular basis, and it may be difficult to believe in something you can't see, but *I* believe that if you're open minded, you *will* see – I believe ESP comes to those who are opened minded. Since a skeptic doesn't believe in ESP, they don't develop it, and they have trouble finding the 'evidence' they're looking for. You might be thinking, 'how the hell does beliving in ESP make it happen to you?', well, remember what I said about thoughts being like a radio? If you 'tune in' to the right station you might find something hors de l'ordinaire ('out of the ordinary').

I feel much more confident about the future than I used to – I definitely feel now that 'things will get better'. If more people stopped to 'contemplate', the world would be more peaceful, and life would become more meaningful - because if there's one thing that makes for a meaningless life, it's war and violence that isn't in a creative form like video games. But if it's a video game about war where they release one a year, and its name is 'Call of Duty', it's probably not the best influence.

Spirituality (as we know it today) is a relatively new thing and there are still so many people who'd be 'in' for spirituality if it made sense to them and wasn't 'a whole lot of New Age terminology' (which you'll notice I've tried to avoid in this book to improve les options d'accessibilité ['accessibility options']).

I once didn't take spirituality seriously at all, but after having these profound experiences, there was no way I was going to stay 'the same old me'. Come to think of it, why would I want to be both 'the same' and 'old' – wouldn't a 'different young me' be better? I consider 'different' to usually be good, it's only if you're a 'Difference Nazi' who can't tolerate anything that's even slightly different that it's a bad thing. Well, we all know what happens to Nazis, don't we?

Even writing this book has felt more spiritual than I was expecting, to borrow a phrase (don't worry, I'll return it – I don't say 'borrow' but really mean 'keep'), writing this book has been 'un voyage' (a journey'). I know, the whole 'it's not the destination, it's the journey' line isn't really anything new, I know I definitely didn't invent it, but I'm realising I've come such a long way.

I used to be slightly sceptical at one point, and there were a lot of things that wouldn't have meant much to me, but now there are many things that it would be easy for some people to dismiss as 'mystical' or 'mumbo jumbo', but I've gained enough of a glimpse of 'another world' that I know now to keep an open mind. Something labelled as 'mystical' or 'mumbo jumbo' actually makes a lot more sense to me now, whereas if I turn on the news and they start talking about 'economics' it makes very *petit* ('little') sense to me.

Some other 'world events' on the news make little sense to me as well, where I'm not able to understand why some of the things on the news happen, and what the people who do some of those things were thinking at the time they did them. Those people who do those terrible things that you hear about on the news (a little too often, unfortunately) seem to possess 'logique absurde' ('nonsensical logic'), and it's almost impossible to imagine how they managed to think it was a good idea – that if they're not insane at the time, they at least have an étrange mentalité ('a strange mentality').

Speaking of 'mystical', some of you skeptics might think the idea of prayer is a strange concept, but 'speaking from experience', I know it definitely makes a difference. I regularly prayer for healing to be sent to certain countries, especially ones that have had a long history of war, and you may be thinking 'why should I consider the idea of prayer ?', but I know it makes a difference. After making these prayers for healing to be sent to those countries (such as Germany, Russia, Middle East), I don't know exactly what effect it has, but I feel a very positive energy afterwards.

This 'positive energy' makes me feel uplifted and I'd describe it as a 'warm feeling inside', or 'waves of joy' as the Beatles' song Across the Universe put it. Compared to *before* sending the healing, *after* sending it I feel more at peace and sorry to sound 'mystical' for a moment, but almost feel a sense of 'Oneness' with the world that I don't feel normally.

To have these feelings specifically after praying for healing to be sent to particular countries suggests that prayer must have some kind of effect. Prayer may sound too 'mystical' if you're a skeptic, but if you ask for something reasonable you'll get a reasonable outcome. What that means is, don't have unrealistic expectations when you pray like 'God, please appear out of nowhere in the middle of a stadium at a Super Bowl to convince people you exist' – because a prayer like this would be unlikely to have a reasonable outcome. In fact, any prayer where you demand 'God' to make some kind of affichage de la puissance ('display of power') to prove his existence is missing the point of prayer and really only shows that you're a skeptic at heart.

I've made many prayers over the last few years, and whenever I pray for healing, either for myself, a particular person, or a particular country, I can feel a changement d'énergie ('energy shift') and almost every time I do, I feel better than I did before the prayer. 'Energy Shift' probably doesn't sound very descriptive, so I'll elaborate.

After praying for these healings, my head will feel lighter, as though a small weight has been taken away from my head, and my mood will be happier and more peaceful. What this does for the people or countries I sometimes pray for healing to be sent to, I can only guess (what's this, guessing? Some 'guru' I am! Oh wait, I didn't *claim* to be a guru to begin with. Just as well, who's heard of a 'guessing guru'?) but I feel much more positive about the future.

I'm much more opened minded than I used to be – now I feel like the only religion that 'resonates' with me is Buddhism, but even that isn't 'all-encompassing' enough for me to call myself a Buddhist.

So what do I call myself if 'Buddhist' isn't 'all-encompassing' enough? I'll share with you where my belief system as it now, which is more of an ouvert à tout ('open to anything') system than a 'belief' system in a strict sense.

I'm not promoting any single viewpoint being completely true or completely false in relation to any other viewpoint, and I'm not saying my belief 'system' is for everyone, I'm only sharing my personal spiritual views and you, the reader are free to agree or disagree with my views. I'm not forcing you (the reader) or anyone or believe or disbelieve anything – you can make your own conclusions, and there aren't necessarily any right or wrong answers.

After having these experiences and becoming 'opened up' to spirituality, I don't consider myself 'religious', I now consider myself a 'Spiritual Communist'. 'What's that? Communist? Aren't they the guys who killed millions of their own people?', you're probably thinking. Actually, you'd be partially wrong – it was totalitarian states that killed millions of their own people, not 'communists', since no country to this day has been a true communist country. I chose the wording 'spiritual communist' because adding 'spiritual' separates it from so-called 'communist' countries that were really only regimes, and because '*commun*ist' has a strong '*commun*ity' aspect. Put the two together, and you get 'a person who is involved within the spiritual community'.

'What the hell is a spiritual community?', you're wondering. Ah, only the most open system ever invented by man. I define a 'spiritual communist' as a person who accepts all true religions of religion and is opposed to dogmatic, extremist, or fundamentalist forms of religion. As an 's.c', I have acceptance for <u>all</u> religions, but not in equal amounts – my 'respect for all religions' operates on somewhat of a sliding scale.

I have the least amount of respect reserved for Christianity (for reasons I won't mention here), followed by Islam (it has a much more developed cosmology, none of that 'fluffy cloud heaven' or 'fire and brimstone hell'. I also agree with their prohibition of alcohol), followed by Zoroastrianism (sadly, a religion that's been almost forgotten. If you've heard of the Mazda car brand, you might be interested in Zoroastrianism), followed by strong acceptance of the Hindu traditions (there seems to be a great body of 'spiritual information' and a deep level of understanding), with the strongest respect and admiration for Buddhism.

I have deep admiration for Buddhism's focus on the Mind, and practicing Mindfulness, which is severely lacking in some parts of the world, where they seem to practice *Mindless*ness instead. I feel Buddhism has much of the same understanding as Hinduism, but in a much more accessible format – Hinduism has a very intellectual understanding of spirituality, while Buddhism focuses on spiritual wisdom rather than spiritual intellectualism. That, and the Dalai Lama makes Buddhism relevant to the Western world like no one before him. Think about it, how many angry Buddhists have you seen?

I have a deep respect for Ancient Wisdom, including spiritual aspects of 'Pagan' traditions (I hesitate to use the word 'Pagan' because of Christian baggage it carries, but in using it, I disregard the aspects related to animal or human sacrifice of worshipping 'demigods' (a Hindu term). There isn't any need to be 'slaves to Elemental Lords',

I disregard anything Pagan relating to 'warrior cultures' such as the Vikings as well, unless that 'warrior culture' is given a modern day reinterpretation and is understood in a *spiritual* sense, rather than a violent sense (or violent sense*less,* because so much of it is*)*. To honour 'Pagan' traditions in the modern day, as a Spiritual Communist would involve 'warrior cultures' such as the Vikings reinventing the definition of a 'warrior', such as a 'crusader of justice', 'champion of 'The People', 'Protector of the Peace' – there's no place in the modern world for culture that celebrates violence as a way of 'entering Heaven'.

It's understandable in ancient terms, people were less sophisticated than in our modern world, but the Pagan traditions had some of the basic ideas – some things were lost in the interpretation of those ideas. I definie the word 'Pagan' as 'Native Tradition' or "Wisdom Tradition' (or 'Native Wisdom Tradition' if you prefer' – while some aspects, like the Vikings' warrior culture are obsolete in the modern world, there are some aspects that can be revived or rebranded, or even reinvented for the modern world.

I strongly reject the notion that Pagan traditions are 'Devil worship', because he would've had to have been an extremely creative Devil. I'm very sceptical about the existence of the 'Devil', at least in the Christian sense – I think it's a lot easier for some people to scapegoat a supposed 'Devil' than to take responsibility for their own actions.

The only concession I'll grant with Pagan traditions and 'Devil worship', is unless 'demigods' have unresolved inner demons, Pagan traditions are not worshipping the 'Christian Devil'. I don't believing in worshipping 'demigods', but even though they had the wrong idea about God in ancient times, we can 'get it right' in modern times. I borrow so much of my understanding of 'Pagan' traditions from Hindu texts, it's a wonder the Hindus seem to have so much more understanding than many of the Pagan traditions in the West.

I'm very open minded towards "New Age' and "Alternative' movements, but I try to avoid using 'New Age Speak' (using a lot of terminology and buzzwords, which means very little to skeptics and atheists, and some religious individuals as well) as much as possible. I consider spirituality to be extremely board and essentially encompassing, to have relatable elements, and to be much more diverse, and beyond labels we might invent like 'Hindu', Buddhist', Zoroastrian', 'Jew', 'Pagan', 'New Age', 'Alternative', etc. I feel that spirituality is all-*in*clusive and non-*ex*clusive.

Even though 'Spiritual Communist' is technically a label as well, I consider it more a concept than a label – it's much better than the 'Spiritual, not Religious' term some people use when they fill out a census ferm. 'Spiritual, not Religious' is far too vague, and it sounds like the people that call themselves that don't fit into any existing category, and themselves aren't actually sure what their 'spiritual views' are and how they'd describe themselves. All it really says about them is that they have an interest in spirituality and don't consider themselves 'religious', other than that it says nothing about what they believe.

To me, 'Spiritual Communist' means someone who is generally and genuinely a 'spiritual seeker' – that you're not limited by factors like culture, religion, gender, having a particular label, etc – it means you're open to anything with elements of spirituality in it, in some cases even things that to the 'average person' would be considered 'obscure'.

Totalitarian regimes that called themselves 'communist' didn't represent the true ideals of communism, whereas as being a 'Spiritual Communist' has a deep spiritual focus.

The phrase 'spiritual communist' to me means that Égalité ('Equality' - racial, gender, religious, ect), liberté ('Liberty' – and not the statue! Just joking. Liberty in the sense of 'Freedoms' in the Human Rights Declaration e.g Freedom of Speech, Freedom of Belief, Freedom of Religion, Freedom of Expression [in its most broad sense of 'any and all forms of creativity', as well as well as the freedom to pursue creative outlets without prejudice or ridicule] etc) and Justice (e.g personal, social, etc), are all very important aspects of spirituality, and without these three things (Equality, Liberty, Justice), you don't have true spirituality.

My entire outlook has life has been dramatically changed (mostly for the better!). I don't hesitate to use the phrase 'life changing experiences', and to say these were 'life changing experiences', would be the understatement of the century (the century so far at least).

I now try to get the most out of life as I can – if I want to see a movie, I don't put it off until the movie's come out on TV, I go see the movie while it's still out and have no regrets about it. I research and buy retro games (mostly RPGs), because there are so many gems I missed out that I either didn't know about or that weren't released here, and I'm rarely disappointed. I read 'alternative books' that I feel drawn to (which I call 'good books', a play on 'The Good Book'), and if I find a new alternative book that I'm drawn to, I'll tell my Mum I've 'found another good book'. Or, if I buy one and she's not home when I come back from the shops and if I manage to finish reading before she gets back, when she gets home, I'll tell her 'I've *read* another good book'

I have a much more Buddhist outlook on life these days – I'm aware of the impermanence of life (in other words, I'm aware that 'death', whatever it is, exists) and these days things like material achievements, education or money I don't see as being the 'be all and end all', and I'm aware of the 'trap' of comparing yourself to other people.

I practice Mindfulness to the best of my ability, to begin with, not being obsédé par l'argent ('obsessed with money') in the first place and by having a realisation of impermanence – that suffering is only temporary.

I try to keep an open mind in relation to 'alternative' or 'New Age' things, such as books, but I understand how their terminology could put so many people off from being spiritual. From my experience (or experiences), spirituality can surprisingly relatable and 'grounded' – the terminology things labelled 'New Age' use can actually distract you from the spirituality components.

I've found that if you know what you're looking for and you don't have any preconceived expectations, you might be surprised what you find. These applies to spirituality, books you might be looking for, video games you might be looking for, or life in general. If you never know what you're looking for, how can you expect to find anything ? To quote Jesus : 'Seek and you shall find'.

'The Spiritual', as in, 'existence other than Matter' is more encompassing than I can describe in words, and even if there are people, especially skeptics, who don't believe in it, it doesn't mean it's not real.

To quote (well, more a slight paraphrase) Shakespeare, 'There are more things in heaven and earth than are dreamt of in your philosophy'.

If Shakespeare could write that hundreds of years ago, then how far have we come since then?

What 'life changing experiences' have you (the reader) had that lead to you becoming more open minded or thinking differently about something that was a long-held view? In particular what experiences have you had that, if you were skeptical before, made you more open to things you hadn't considered, or to possibilities you once thought impossible?

Use the following blank pages to record 'Life Changing Experiences' (in pencil – or on a separate sheet of paper if you want to write in pen) – you can show other people or keep it to yourself, it's your choice. Write a brief description of the event, then write how it changed your life – it can be as simple or detailed as you choose.

Longue vie et prospérité. Look that one up and see if you get the reference.

Je l'espère, ce livre vous a aidé ('I hope this book has helped you'). Je vous dis adieu ! ('I bid you adieu!')

www.ingramcontent.com/pod-product-compliance
Lightning Source LLC
Chambersburg PA
CBHW031409040426
42444CB00005B/482